Developing Nations

Other Books in the Current Controversies Series

Developing Nations

Debra A. Miller, Book Editor

GREENHAVEN PRESS

An imprint of Thomson Gale, a part of The Thomson Corporation

Detroit • New York • San Francisco • New Haven, Conn. • Waterville, Maine • London

Christine Nasso, *Publisher*
Elizabeth Des Chenes, *Managing Editor*

For more information, contact:
Greenhaven Press
27500 Drake Rd.
Farmington Hills, MI 48331-3535
Or you can visit our Internet site at http://www.gale.com

LIBRARY OF CONGRESS CATALOGING-IN-PUBLICATION DATA

Developing nations / Debra A. Miller, book editor.
   p. cm. -- (Current controversies)
   Includes bibliographical references and index.
   ISBN-13: 978-0-7377-3713-4 (hardcover)
   ISBN-13: 978-0-7377-3714-1 (pbk.)
   1. Developing countries--Economic conditions--21st century. 2. Developing countries--Social conditions--21st century. 3. Globalization--Economic aspects --Developing countries. 4. Globalization--Social aspects--Developing countries. 5. Globalization--Moral and ethical aspects--Developing countries.
   I. Miller, Debra A.
   HC59.7.D427 2007
   330.9172'4--dc22
                                                                2007018369

ISBN-10: 0-7377-3713-1 (hardcover)
ISBN-10: 0-7377-3714-X (pbk.)

Contents

No: Democracy Cannot Succeed in Developing Nations

Chapter 4: How Should Industrialized Nations Aid the Developing World?

Foreword

By definition, controversies are "discussions of questions in which opposing opinions clash" (Webster's Twentieth Century Dictionary Unabridged). Few would deny that controversies are a pervasive part of the human condition and exist on virtually every level of human enterprise. Controversies transpire between individuals and among groups, within nations and between nations. Controversies supply the grist necessary for progress by providing challenges and challengers to the status quo. They also create atmospheres where strife and warfare can flourish. A world without controversies would be a peaceful world; but it also would be, by and large, static and prosaic.

The Series' Purpose

The purpose of the Current Controversies series is to explore many of the social, political, and economic controversies dominating the national and international scenes today. Titles selected for inclusion in the series are highly focused and specific. For example, from the larger category of criminal justice, Current Controversies deals with specific topics such as police brutality, gun control, white collar crime, and others. The debates in Current Controversies also are presented in a useful, timeless fashion. Articles and book excerpts included in each title are selected if they contribute valuable, long-range ideas to the overall debate. And wherever possible, current information is enhanced with historical documents and other relevant materials. Thus, while individual titles are current in focus, every effort is made to ensure that they will not become quickly outdated. Books in the Current Controversies series will remain important resources for librarians, teachers, and students for many years.

In addition to keeping the titles focused and specific, great care is taken in the editorial format of each book in the series. Book introductions and chapter prefaces are offered to provide background material for readers. Chapters are organized around several key questions that are answered with diverse opinions representing all points on the political spectrum. Materials in each chapter include opinions in which authors clearly disagree as well as alternative opinions in which authors may agree on a broader issue but disagree on the possible solutions. In this way, the content of each volume in Current Controversies mirrors the mosaic of opinions encountered in society. Readers will quickly realize that there are many viable answers to these complex issues. By questioning each author's conclusions, students and casual readers can begin to develop the critical thinking skills so important to evaluating opinionated material.

Current Controversies is also ideal for controlled research. Each anthology in the series is composed of primary sources taken from a wide gamut of informational categories including periodicals, newspapers, books, U.S. and foreign government documents, and the publications of private and public organizations. Readers will find factual support for reports, debates, and research papers covering all areas of important issues. In addition, an annotated table of contents, an index, a book and periodical bibliography, and a list of organizations to contact are included in each book to expedite further research.

Perhaps more than ever before in history, people are confronted with diverse and contradictory information. During the Persian Gulf War, for example, the public was not only treated to minute-to-minute coverage of the war, it was also inundated with critiques of the coverage and countless analyses of the factors motivating U.S. involvement. Being able to sort through the plethora of opinions accompanying today's major issues, and to draw one's own conclusions, can be a complicated and frustrating struggle. It is the editors' hope that Current Controversies will help readers with this struggle.

Introduction

> *"Celebrities, high-profile business leaders, and politicians have banded together to find solutions to some of the most difficult problems facing the developing world."*

The first decade of the twenty-first century has witnessed a new phenomenon that some have called a new age of philanthropy—a time in which celebrities, high-profile business leaders, and politicians have banded together to find solutions to some of the most difficult problems facing the developing world. The result of this collaboration has been a significant increase in the amount of aid available to developing countries from both private and government sources, improving the budgets for battling intractable global problems such as poverty and disease.

Some commentators attribute this heightened world consciousness to improvements in information technology that allow people in rich countries to see the suffering taking place in poor nations, creating a much greater level of awareness and humanitarian concern. Today, unlike in the past, twenty-four-hour global news stations beam images of the victims of disasters, wars, and disease into our homes daily, and Internet communications allow for an even quicker dissemination of news and information. Acquisition of astronomical wealth by certain individuals in rich countries also allows private philanthropy to reach record levels that have never been possible before now. Middle-income people in wealthy nations, too, have seen increases in their standards of living that allow them to make charitable giving a routine part of their yearly expenditures.

One of the biggest private philanthropists, for example, is the Bill and Melinda Gates Foundation, a charitable organization created and endowed by the founder of Microsoft, the world's leading computer software company. Since it was funded with an initial $5 billion in 1999, the foundation has poured its resources into global health and other causes. Between 2000 and 2005, for example, the Gates Foundation donated well over a billion dollars to various health efforts, including $150 million to the Global Fund to Fight AIDS, Tuberculosis and Malaria, and more than $100 million to help children suffering from AIDS in India. In 2005, the foundation donated a massive $750 million to launch the Global Alliance for Vaccines and Immunizations, a coalition of international public health agencies, philanthropists, and drug companies created to develop and deliver vaccines for various diseases, including AIDS, tuberculosis, and malaria. By 2005, the foundation had an endowment of about $29 billion, and was expected to donate at least $1 billion annually to global health causes.

In 2006, however, the Gates endowment mushroomed in size when one of the world's richest men, seventy-five-year-old Warren Buffett announced that he would give away more than $37 billion of his $40 billion fortune, most of it to the Gates Foundation. Buffett's 2006 donation to the fund alone roughly doubled the foundation's budget for that year. Buffett's annual endowment is expected to increase as Buffett's stock rises in value, so that the actual value of the overall donation is not yet discernible. Even at current value, however, Buffett's donation is by far the largest private philanthropic gift in history.

However, private philanthropy cannot match the impact that government aid can have on development problems. As Bill Gates has said, "No foundation alone can solve the . . . problems of the developing world. We need businesses and governments as partners." Helping to encourage greater government spending is the focus of another of the influential new celebrity philanthropists—Paul David Hewson, known as Bono, the lead singer of the Irish rock band U2. In 2002, for example, Bono set up an organization called DATA (Debt, AIDS, Trade, Africa) to raise awareness about AIDS and other problems facing the region. Bono also has been highly successful at pressuring governments to forgive debt and increase their foreign aid to all developing countries. In 2005, Bono's efforts encouraged the world's richest countries to forgive $40 billion in debt owed by the poorest nations—a decision that gave many developing nations the ability to spend more of their scanty resources on critical problems such as poverty and health.

In January 2006, Bono launched a new partnership with American Express and other companies aimed at funding the Global Fund to Fight AIDS, Tuberculosis and Malaria, an international organization devoted to global health issues. That same year Bono also helped initiate the ONE campaign, an effort to convince U.S. officials to allocate an additional 1 percent of the U.S. budget toward providing basic needs for developing countries. The campaign calls for debt cancellation, trade reform, and anticorruption measures to be directed toward Africa and the world's poorest nations to help them conquer AIDS and extreme poverty. In recognition of their tremendous impact in the developing world, *Time* magazine named Bill and Melinda Gates, along with Bono, "persons of the year" in 2005.

Other charismatic public figures have also contributed to the efforts to increase aid to the developing world. Former presidents Bill Clinton and George H.W. Bush, for example, raised large sums for the victims of the deadly tsunami that struck Indonesia, Thailand, and Sri Lanka in December 2004. Their efforts inspired the U.S. government to pledge $350 million in tsunami aid and raised more than $10 million from private sources. Clinton also has established the William J.

Clinton Foundation, a charitable group that focuses on providing aid and attention to four issues important to developing countries: health; economic empowerment; leadership development and citizen service; and racial, ethnic, and religious reconciliation.

Many observers hope that this attention to the problems of the developing world will make a major change in the lives of billions of the world's poorest citizens. The authors in *Current Controversies: Developing Nations* help to explain this monumental challenge by giving their perspectives on the specific problems faced by developing nations. The selections also cover the effect of globalization and democratization in the developing world, and various other strategies being proposed for solving the problems of poor and developing nations.

CHAPTER 1

What Are the Problems Facing Developing Nations?

Chapter Preface

The world's developing nations face many challenges, such as extreme poverty, hunger and malnutrition, rampant disease and ill health, and environmental pollution, but many of these problems are closely related to a lack of revenue caused by underdevelopment of their economies. In recent decades, some poor countries have successfully begun to expand their economies, only to encounter a new problem—global warming. Manufacturing and other industries critical to economic development in developing countries are often dependent on energy derived from fossil fuels such as oil, gas, and coal that produce so-called greenhouse gases, including carbon dioxide, methane, nitrogen oxides, sulfur hexafluoride, haloalkanes (HFCs), and perfluorocarbons (PFCs). These greenhouse emissions trap the sun's energy in the Earth's atmosphere and, over time, are causing a slow rise in average temperatures around the globe.

This changing world climate is one of the most debated environmental problems of the new millennium. Experts have warned that global warming may have serious costs: Agriculture and fisheries could be decimated; climate fluctuations may cause severe weather changes, such as increased rains and hurricanes in some areas and droughts in others; and rising sea levels may wipe out coastal cities, beaches, wetlands, and even large tracts of dry land. In addition, temperature changes could spread tropical diseases to new regions, and many animal and plant species may become extinct.

These changes could be devastating to developing countries that simply do not have the resources or technology to respond to rising sea levels, destructive weather patterns, or new diseases. Developing nations are therefore caught in a terrible bind—they desperately need rapid economic development, yet pursuing that goal could bring a whole new set of problems, not only for themselves but for the entire planet. Many commentators point out that this is an unfair burden for the developing world, because poor nations only want to do what the developed nations of the world have been doing for the last hundred years—growing their economies as fast as possible without restriction. In fact, most of the carbon and other harmful greenhouse gases that are contributing to today's global warming problem were produced by the burning of oil and coal in highly developed regions such as the United States, Canada, Europe, Australia, and Japan. The United States alone is reportedly responsible for at least 25 percent of those greenhouse emissions.

So far, the main international response to this threat of global warming has been the Kyoto Protocol, part of the United Nations Framework Convention on Climate Change (UNFCCC), an international treaty on global warming. The Kyoto portions of the treaty set mandatory targets for the reduction of greenhouse gases, with the goal of encouraging industrialized countries to reduce their total emissions of major greenhouse gases by 5.2 percent over the five-year period of 2008–2012.

The Kyoto agreement, however, has run into many obstacles and is not expected to solve the global warming problem. Many signatory countries are having difficulty meeting their Kyoto goals, and some major greenhouse gas emitters, such as the United States and Australia, have refused to ratify or comply with the treaty. Also, some experts say the Kyoto goals, even if met, will be insufficient to stop or significantly slow global warming. In addition, disagreements have erupted about exempting developing countries from mandatory Kyoto emissions reductions. The United States, for example, declined to ratify Kyoto because it did not apply to developing countries, arguing that this would place the U.S. companies at a disadvantage and harm the U.S. economy. U.S. officials and many other observers worry that rapid development in countries such as China and India will result in an uncontrolled spike of carbon emissions that will offset any hard-won future reductions achieved by the developed world.

Many experts have concluded that the best solution is for all nations to take immediate steps to reduce their heavy reliance on oil, gas, and coal fuels. These steps could include aggressive energy efficiency programs, efforts to reduce deforestation and plant more trees (which are known to reduce carbon in the atmosphere), and clean energy alternatives to fossil fuels. Already, renewable, nonpolluting energy technologies such as solar, wind, geothermal, and tidal power have shown great potential, and many people think they could eventually replace fossil fuels completely if sufficient resources were committed to promoting their development.

The transition from a fossil fuel–powered world to one fueled by new, clean energy sources, however, will require significant new expenditures, perhaps as much as $5 trillion, according to some estimates. Many poor countries simply cannot afford to divert their scarce resources away from current priorities, which are to promote economic development rather than environmental policies. Many experts conclude, therefore, that wealthier, industrialized countries must lead the way to a cleaner energy future. Germany is already at the forefront of this transition. It passed the Renewable Energy Law in 2000 that requires the nation's electric utilities to buy renewable power such as wind and solar, and subsidizes the development of those alternative energy companies. The result has been a significant increase in the growth of the renewable energy market in the country and an accompanying reduction of carbon emissions. Developed countries can also benefit directly from funding programs to prevent deforestation and promote new energy technologies in the developing world. The Kyoto treaty, for example, contains the Clean Development Mechanism (CDM), which allows developed countries to earn carbon credits for projects in developing countries that reduce greenhouse gases; developed nations can then apply these credits toward their Kyoto emissions goals.

If developed nations embrace this transition, global warming may one day no longer be a threat anywhere in the world. Today, however, global warming presents a major challenge, particularly for poor countries. The viewpoints in this chapter discuss some of the other serious problems facing the developing world.

Poverty Is a Serious Problem in Developing Nations

World Summit on Sustainable Development

World Summit on Sustainable Development was a meeting of global leaders held in Johannesburg, South Africa, in 2002, resulting in a plan of implementation containing thirty environmental protection goals.

There are 1.2 billion people living on less than one dollar a day, and about half the world's population lives on less than two dollars a day. With few choices or opportunities, they are condemned to lives that are prone to hunger, disease, illiteracy, joblessness and hopelessness. Too often, they lack access to food, safe drinking water, sanitation, education, health care and modern energy services.

At the Millennium Summit in September 2000, 147 heads of State and Government and 191 nations in total adopted the Millennium Declaration, which set out specific targets for development and poverty eradication. By 2015, they pledged to:

Reduce by half the proportion of people living on less than a dollar a day.

Reduce by half the proportion of people who suffer from hunger.

Reduce by half the proportion of people without access to safe and affordable drinking water.

Ensure that all boys and girls complete a full course of primary schooling.

Achieve gender equality in access to education.

World Summit on Sustainable Development, "Facts about Poverty and the Millennium Development Goals," August 25–September 4, 2002. www.johannesburgsummit.org. Reproduced by permission.

Reduce by three quarters the maternal mortality rate.

Reduce by two thirds the mortality rate among children under five.

Halt and begin to reverse the spread of HIV/AIDS, malaria and other major diseases.

Achieve significant improvement in the lives of at least 100 million slum dwellers, by 2020.

Key Statistics

While there are substantial numbers of people living in poverty in developed countries, most of the people living in extreme poverty reside in developing countries. Of the 4.6 billion people in developing countries:

Almost 800 million are not getting enough food to lead normal, healthy and active lives.

More than 850 million are illiterate.

More than one billion people lack access to clean water supplies.

Some 2.4 billion lack access to basic sanitation.

Nearly 325 million boys and girls are not in school.

11 million children under the age of five die each year from preventable causes.

Around 36 million people are living with HIV/AIDS.

Around 120 million couples who want to use contraception do not have access to it.

East Asia's poverty rate has fallen from about 28 per cent in 1990 to 15 per cent in 1998, with the number of people living in poverty declining from 418 million to 267 million. In sub-Saharan Africa, the poverty rate is about 48 per cent and has remained unchanged over the last decade. However, the number of people living in poverty has grown, from 220 million in 1990 to 300 million in 1998.

What Needs to Be Done

Progress is possible. Already, there has been success in increasing the average life expectancy worldwide from 60 to 70 years; the infant mortality rate has dropped from 100 to 50 per thousand live births; the number of undernourished declined from roughly 900 million to about 800 million; and the adult literacy rate is up, from slightly over 60 per cent to nearly 80 per cent. The share of rural families in developing countries with access to safe water has grown more than fivefold within the past 30 years and contraceptive prevalence has reached nearly 50 per cent in developing countries.

Despite . . . advances, poverty on the global scale continues.

Through trade and investment and reforms in other areas such as finance, governance, infrastructure and legal systems, countries that successfully integrated into the world economy saw per-capita income grow up to 5 per cent per year in the 1990s. Growth in countries such as China, India, Uganda and Vietnam has driven a global reduction in the poverty rate. In the 1990s China reduced the number of people living in extreme poverty from 360 million to 210 million. In Uganda poverty fell 40 per cent, and in Vietnam it fell by half. Many developing countries have already achieved universal primary education for both boys and girls, or are on track to do so. Over 60 per cent of the world's people live in 43 countries that have met or are on track to meet the goal of reducing by half the proportion of people who go hungry.

Despite these advances, poverty on the global scale continues. [The] United Nations Secretary-General ... has called on donor countries to almost double present levels of assistance, to $100 billion a year, in order to meet the Millennium Summit Goals. The World Bank, in a report released in January 2002, came up with similar results, calculating that additional aid of $40-$60 billion a year would be needed to reach the Goals. [Former] World Bank President James Wolfensohn said that would be roughly a doubling of current aid flows, to approximately 0.5 per cent of gross national product for developed countries—still well below the 0.7 per cent target agreed by global leaders years ago. In response to this call from the United Nations and others, an additional $12 billion a year in aid by 2006 was pledged by world leaders at the International Conference on Financing for Development, held in Monterrey, Mexico, in March 2002. Although the totals pledged did not meet the levels needed, they reversed the trend of declining aid.... [As of January 2007, a few countries had met or exceeded those commitments, while many countries' aid levels remained substantially below the 0.7 percent goal.] How to generate additional funds and how best to direct aid in order to achieve sustainable development are [the] key [remaining] challenges.

Hunger and Malnutrition Are the Oldest Enemies of Developing Countries

United Nations World Food Programme

The United Nations World Food Programme is the food aid arm of the United Nations that seeks to eliminate global poverty and hunger.

Hunger and malnutrition are still the number one risks to health worldwide. In the final quarter of the 20th century, humanity was winning the war on its oldest enemy. From 1970–1997, the number of hungry people dropped from 959 million to 791 million—mainly the result of dramatic progress in reducing the number of undernourished in China and India. In the second half of the 1990s, however, the number of chronically hungry in developing countries increased at a rate of almost four million per year. By 2000–2002, the total number of undernourished people worldwide had risen to 852 million: 815 million in developing countries, 28 million in countries in transition and nine million in industrialised countries. Today, one in nearly seven people do not get enough food to be healthy and lead an active life, making hunger and malnutrition the number one risk to health worldwide—greater than AIDS, malaria and tuberculosis combined.

Acute Hunger and Undernourishment

Acute hunger or starvation are often highlighted on TV screens: hungry mothers too weak to breastfeed their children in drought-hit Ethiopia, refugees in war-torn Democratic Republic of Congo queueing for food rations, helicopters airlifting high energy biscuits to flood victims marooned in Bang-

United Nations World Food Programme, "Hunger, Humanity's Oldest Enemy," 2006. www.wfp.org. Reproduced by permission.

ladesh or Cambodia. Such dramatic images are the result of high profile crises like war or natural disasters, which starve a population of food. But emergencies account for just eight percent of hunger's victims.

Daily undernourishment is a less visible form of hunger—but it affects many more people, from the shanty towns of Jakarta in Indonesia and the Cambodian capital Phnom Penh to the mountain villages of Bolivia and Nepal. In these places, hunger is much more than an empty stomach. . . . For weeks, even months, its victims must live on significantly less than the recommended 2,100 calories that the average person needs to lead a healthy life.

The body compensates for the lack of energy by slowing down its physical and mental activities. A hungry mind cannot concentrate, a hungry body does not take initiative, a hungry child loses all desire to play and study. Hunger also weakens the immune system. Deprived of the right nutrition, hungry children are especially vulnerable and become too weak to fight off disease and may die from common infections like measles and diarrhea. Each year, malnutrition contributes to the deaths of an estimated 10 million under-fives.

Hunger not only weighs heavily on the individual. It imposes a crushing economic burden on the developing world.

Malnutrition

Labelled as the largest single contributor to disease by the UN's standing committee on nutrition, malnutrition is the result of inadequate dietary intake, infection, or both. It is more about quality than quantity of food. Even if people get enough to eat, they will become malnourished if the food does not provide the proper amounts of micronutrients—vitamins and minerals—to meet daily nutritional requirements.

Each form of malnutrition depends on what nutrients are missing in the diet, for how long and at what age. The most basic kind is called protein energy deficiency. It results from a diet lacking in energy and protein because of a deficit in all major macronutrients, such as carbohydrates, fats and proteins. Marasmus is caused by a lack of protein and energy and can lead to atrophy or kwashiorkor. Other forms of malnutrition are less visible—but no less deadly. They are usually the result of vitamin and mineral deficiencies (micronutrients), which can lead to anaemia, scurvy, pellagra, beriberi and xeropthalmia.

According to the Food and Agriculture Organization's (FAO) 2004 Food Insecurity Report, vitamin and mineral deficiencies afflict nearly two billion people worldwide. Deficiencies of iron, vitamin A and zinc are ranked among the World Health Organization's (WHO) top 10 leading causes of death through disease in developing countries:

- *Iron deficiency* is the most prevalent form of malnutrition worldwide, affecting an estimated 1.7 billion people, half of whom suffer from anaemia. Iron forms the molecules that carry oxygen in the blood, so symptoms of a deficiency include tiredness and lethargy. Lack of iron in large segments of the population severely damages a country's productivity. Iron deficiency also impedes cognitive development, affecting 40–60 percent of children in developing countries.

- *Vitamin A deficiency* weakens the immune systems of a large proportion of under-fives in poor countries, increasing their vulnerability to disease. A deficiency in vitamin A, for example, increases the risk of dying from diarrhea, measles and malaria by 20–24 percent. Affecting 140 million preschool children in 118 countries and more than seven million pregnant women, it is also a leading cause of child blindness across developing countries.

- *Iodine deficiency* affects 780 million people worldwide. The clearest symptom is a swelling of the thyroid gland called a goitre. But the most serious impact is on the brain, which cannot develop properly without iodine. According to UN research, some 20 million children are born mentally impaired because their mothers did not consume enough iodine. The worst-hit suffer cretinism, associated with severe mental retardation and physical stunting.

- *Zinc deficiency* contributes to growth failure and weakened immunity in young children. It is linked to a higher risk of diarrhea and pneumonia, resulting in some 800,000 deaths per year.

Global Cost of Hunger

Hunger not only weighs heavily on the individual. It imposes a crushing economic burden on the developing world. Economists estimate that every child whose physical and mental development is stunted by hunger and malnutrition stands to lose five to 10 percent in lifetime earnings.

There is enough food available to feed the entire global population of 6.4 billion people. And yet, one in nearly seven people are going hungry.

Disability-adjusted years or DALYs measure the number of years lost as a result both of premature death and of disabilities, adjusted for severity. According to the 2004 FAO Food Insecurity Report, childhood and maternal undernutrition cost an estimated 220 million DALYs in developing countries. When other nutrition-related risk factors are taken into account, the toll rises to 340 million DALYs—equivalent to having a disaster kill or disable the entire population of a country larger than the United States.

Why Does Hunger Exist?

Food has never before existed in such abundance, so why are 815 million people in developing countries going hungry? In purely quantitative terms, there is enough food available to feed the entire global population of 6.4 billion people. And yet, one in nearly seven people are going hungry. One in three children are underweight. Why does hunger exist?

Natural disasters such as floods, tropical storms and long periods of drought are on the increase—with calamitous consequences for food security in poor, developing countries. Drought is now the single most common cause of food shortages in the world. In 2004, recurrent drought caused crop failures and heavy livestock losses in parts of Ethiopia, Eritrea, Somalia, Uganda and Kenya. In many countries, climate change is exacerbating already adverse natural conditions. For example, poor farmers in Ethiopia or Guatemala traditionally deal with rain failure by selling off livestock to cover their losses and pay for food. But successive years of drought, increasingly common in the Horn of Africa and Central America, are exhausting their resources.

Since 1992, the proportion of short and long-term food crises that can be attributed to human causes has more than doubled, rising from 15 percent to more than 35 percent. All too often, these emergencies are triggered by conflict. From Asia to Africa to Latin America, fighting displaces millions of people from their homes, leading to some of the world's worst hunger emergencies. In 2004, escalating conflict in the Darfur region of Sudan uprooted more than a million people, precipitating a major food crisis—in an area that had generally enjoyed good rains and crops.

In war, food sometimes becomes a weapon. Soldiers will starve opponents into submission by seizing or destroying food and livestock and systematically wrecking local markets. Fields and water wells are often mined or contaminated, forcing farmers to abandon their land. When conflict threw Central Africa into confusion in the 1990s, the proportion of hungry people rose from 53 percent to 58 percent. By comparision, malnutrition is on the retreat in more peaceful parts of Africa such as Ghana and Malawi. . . .

In developing countries, farmers often cannot afford seed to plant the crops that would provide for their families. Craftsmen lack the means to pay for the tools to ply their trade. Others have no land or water or education to lay the foundations for a secure future. The poverty-stricken do not have enough money to buy or produce enough food for themselves and their families. In turn, they tend to be weaker and cannot produce enough to buy more food. In short, the poor are hungry and their hunger traps them in poverty. . . .

In the long-term, improved agricultural output offers the quickest fix for poverty and hunger. According to the Food and Agriculture Organization (FAO) 2004 Food Insecurity Report, all the countries that are on track to reach the first Millennium Development Goal have something in common— significantly better than average agricultural growth. Yet too many developing countries lack key agricultural infrastructure, such as enough roads, warehouses and irrigation. The results are high transport costs, lack of storage facilities and unreliable water supplies. All conspire to limit agricultural yields and access to food. But, although the majority of developing countries depend on agriculture, their governments' economic planning often emphasises urban development.

There are over 800 million hungry people in developing countries . . . more than the combined populations of the United States, Canada and the European Union.

Poor farming practices, deforestation, overcropping and overgrazing are exhausting the Earth's fertility and spreading the roots of hunger. Increasingly, the world's fertile farmland is under threat from erosion, salination and desertification.

Faces of the Hungry

Ten million people die every year of hunger and hunger-related diseases. Only eight percent are the victims of high-profile earthquakes, floods, droughts and wars. The rest are often forgotten. Who are they?

Ask about the hungry and most people will talk about the victims of Ethiopia's famine in 1984–85, homeless families marooned by Bangladeshi floods or refugees fleeing war in the Democratic Republic of Congo.

They probably won't know that in total there are over 800 million hungry people in developing countries who don't make the headlines—more than the combined populations of the United States, Canada and the European Union. They come at all ages, from babies whose mothers cannot produce enough milk to the elderly with no relatives to care for them. They are the unemployed inhabitants of urban slums, the landless farmers tilling other peoples' fields, the orphans of AIDS and the sick, who need special or increased food intake to survive.

The scales are tipped against the vast majority of the world's hungry from birth. Over 20 million low birthweight (LBW) babies are born in developing countries every year. Even if they survive infancy, LBW babies face stunted physical and cognitive growth in childhood. As adults, this translates into reduced work capacity and earnings. Hunger's vicious cycle not only extends throughout the victim's lifetime but also into the next generation. Malnourished mothers give birth to LBW babies.

Rural Risk

Three-quarters of all hungry people live in rural areas, mainly in the villages of Asia and Africa. Overwhelmingly dependent on agriculture for their food, these populations have no alternative source of income or employment and, as a result, are particularly vulnerable to crises. Many migrate to cities in their search for employment, swelling the ever-expanding populations of shanty towns in developing countries.

The Food and Agriculture Organization (FAO) calculates that of the developing countries' 815 million hungry, half are farming families, surviving off marginal lands prone to natural disasters like drought or flood, and one in five belong to landless families dependent on farming. About 10 percent live in communities whose livelihoods depend on herding, fishing or forest resources. The remaining 25 percent live in shanty towns on the periphery of the biggest cities in developing countries. The numbers of poor and hungry city dwellers are rising rapidly along with the world's total urban population. A study of 14 developing countries by the International Food Policy Research Institute showed that, from 1985-1996, the number of underweight children living in urban areas rose at a more rapid rate than in rural areas.

Child Hunger and Women

An estimated 167 million children under five years of age in the world are underweight—the result of acute or chronic hunger. This means that 20 percent of all hungry people are children aged less than five. All too often, child hunger is inherited: up to 17 million children are born underweight annually, the result of inadequate nutrition before and during pregnancy. Undernourished infants lose their curiosity, motivation and even the will to play. Millions leave school prematurely.

Chronic hunger also delays or stops the physical and mental growth of children. Poor or insufficient nutrition over time means some 226 million children are too small for their age. Most tragically, diseases such as measles or dysentery, can kill undernourished children. According to the FAO, every year that hunger continues at present levels costs five million children their lives. In adult life, child hunger gnaws away at the productivity of entire countries' workforces. Economists estimate hunger is responsible for reducing the GNP [gross national product] of some developing countries by two to four percent. . . .

Women are the world's primary food producers, yet cultural traditions and social structures often mean women are much more affected by hunger and poverty than men. Seven out of 10 of the world's hungry are women and girls.

While around 25 percent of men in developing countries suffer from anaemia caused by an iron deficiency, 45 percent of women are affected. Lack of iron means 300 women die during childbirth every day. As a result, women, in particular, expectant and nursing mothers, often need special or increased intake of food. Maternal stunting and underweight are also among the most prevalent causes of giving birth to a low birthweight child.

Lack of Health Funding Causes Millions to Die in Developing Countries Each Year

Pharmaceutical Research and Manufacturers of America

The Pharmaceutical Research and Manufacturers of America (PhRMA) represents the country's leading pharmaceutical research and biotechnology companies.

AIDS is only one of numerous infectious diseases that affect the developing world. Also afflicting the world's poor is the condition of their countries' infrastructures and public health systems. That and other factors (such as famine and war) complicate efforts in the developing world to fight lethal diseases and maintain good health. The World Health Organization (WHO) provides grim numbers:

- Acute Respiratory Infections such as influenza and pneumonia kill about 4 million people annually, a disproportionate number of them in the world's poorest nations.

- Diarrheal Diseases such as cholera, dysentery, typhoid fever and rotavirus claim roughly two million small children annually, virtually all of them are from developing nations.

- Tuberculosis kills 1.7 million people a year, mostly in Africa and Southeast Asia.

- Malaria kills 3,000 people a day and more than one million each year, most of them young children and most of them in sub-Saharan Africa.

Pharmaceutical Research and Manufacturers of America, "Infectious Diseases Besiege Poor Nations," 2006. http://world.phrma.org. Reproduced by permission.

- Measles is responsible for 900,000 deaths a year in developing nations.

- HIV/AIDS claims 3 million to 4 million lives each year, up to 2.3 million in Africa. Of the 14,000 new infections each day, 95 percent are in developing nations.

Battling Disease

The public health systems of the developing world are grossly underfunded.

- In its 2002 report, the Commission on Macroeconomics and Health, headed by economist Jeffrey Sachs and sponsored by the WHO, found that health care spending in the poorest countries is about $57 billion short of the minimum needed for good basic care.

- WHO recently ranked the national health systems of developing nations near the bottom in almost every measure. Trained health workers are in short supply. Hospitals are dilapidated and crowded—in many places, AIDS patients lie two to a bed. Facilities and providers are often concentrated in cities.

- Many medical therapies are out of reach. One-third of the world's population do not have access to drugs on the WHO's Essential Drug List, a fraction that has hardly changed in decades. Alas, many low-cost preventive therapies and medicines, many long off patent and available generically, are [still too expensive for developing nations.]

- Developing countries must spend $60 per capita a year to meet the most basic health care needs—which doesn't include battling AIDS and other difficult health challenges. Yet scores of nations spend less, some less than $20 per capita. . . .

Developing nations struggle mightily with poor infrastructure, unsafe water, famine, malnutrition and lack of refrigeration. Poor transportation makes health care virtually inaccessible for large portions of the population in the developing world. But money is not the only issue. Many developing world governments underfund health care, either because of politics, mismanagement or worse.

Pharmaceutical Industry Efforts

Between 1998 and 2001, the [pharmaceutical] industry provided developing countries more than $1.9 billion in financial assistance and donated medicines, including $564 million in 2001 alone.

- Working with local NGOs [nongovernmental organizations] and international health and relief groups, the industry helped train health workers and build and equip clinics.

- Initiatives also include free flu vaccinations for 3 million children, 10 million doses of oral polio vaccine, an anti-trachoma program to combat preventable blindness, health and hygiene education, and water purification programs.

- In May 2000 five pharmaceutical companies and the U.N. [United Nations] established the Accelerating Access Initiative, a program that offers AIDS medicines at or below cost and in some cases for free.

Clearly, these efforts are just a partial solution. A boost in health care spending of one percent GDP [gross domestic product] by developing nations themselves would raise only about 60 percent of the amount needed for good basic care. The world community would have to fund the balance.

Air and Water
Pollution Plague Poor,
Developing Countries

The Economist

The Economist is a British newsmagazine that focuses on world economic issues.

Why should we care about the environment? Ask a European, and he will probably point to global warming. Ask the two little boys playing outside a newsstand in Da Shilan, a shabby neighbourhood in the heart of Beijing, [China,] and they will tell you about the city's notoriously foul air: "It's bad—like a virus!"

Given all the media coverage in the rich world, people there might believe that global scares are the chief environmental problems facing humanity today. They would be wrong. Partha Dasgupta, an economics professor at Cambridge University, thinks the current interest in global, future-oriented problems has "drawn attention away from the economic misery and ecological degradation endemic in large parts of the world today. Disaster is not something for which the poorest have to wait; it is a frequent occurrence."

Environmental Problems in Developing Countries

Every year in developing countries, a million people die from urban air pollution and twice that number from exposure to stove smoke inside their homes. Another 3m [3 million] unfortunates die prematurely every year from water-related diseases. All told, premature deaths and illnesses arising from environmental factors account for about a fifth of all diseases in poor countries, bigger than any other preventable factor, including malnutrition. The problem is so serious that Ian Johnson, the World Bank's vice-president for the environment, tells his colleagues, with a touch of irony, that he is really the bank's vice-president for health: "I say tackling the underlying environmental causes of health problems will do a lot more good than just more hospitals and drugs."

Environmental risks (such as water-borne diseases) cause far more health problems in poor countries than modern environmental risks (such as industrial pollution).

The link between environment and poverty is central to that great race for sustainability. It is a pity, then, that several powerful fallacies keep getting in the way of sensible debate. One popular myth is that trade and economic growth make poor countries' environmental problems worse. Growth, it is said, brings with it urbanisation, higher energy consumption and industrialisation—all factors that contribute to pollution and pose health risks. In a static world, that would be true, because every new factory causes extra pollution. But in the real world, economic growth unleashes many dynamic forces that, in the longer run, more than offset that extra pollution. . . . Traditional environmental risks (such as water-borne diseases) cause far more health problems in poor countries than modern environmental risks (such as industrial pollution).

Economic Growth and Pollution

However, this is not to say that trade and economic growth will solve all environmental problems. Among the reasons for doubt are the "perverse" conditions under which world trade is carried on, argues Oxfam. The British charity thinks the rules of trade are "unfairly rigged against the poor," and cites in evidence the enormous subsidies lavished by rich countries on industries such as agriculture, as well as trade protection offered to manufacturing industries such as textiles. These measures hurt the environment because they force the world's poorest countries to rely heavily on commodities—a particularly energy-intensive and ungreen sector.

Mr. Dasgupta argues that this distortion of trade amounts to a massive subsidy of rich-world consumption paid by the world's poorest people. The most persuasive critique of all goes as follows: "Economic growth is not sufficient for turning environmental degradation around. If economic incentives facing producers and consumers do not change with higher incomes, pollution will continue to grow unabated with the growing scale of economic activity." Those words come not from some anti-globalist green group, but from the World Trade Organisation.

Intelligent government policies might well help to reduce pollution even while countries are still relatively poor.

Another common view is that poor countries, being unable to afford greenery [i.e., environmentally friendly policies], should pollute now and clean up later. Certainly poor countries should not be made to adopt American or European environmental standards. But there is evidence to suggest that poor countries can and should try to tackle some environmental problems now, rather than wait till they have become richer.

This so-called "smart growth" strategy contradicts conventional wisdom. For many years, economists have observed that as agrarian societies industrialised, pollution increased at first, but as the societies grew wealthier it declined again. The trouble is that this applies only to some pollutants, such as sulphur dioxide, but not to others, such as carbon dioxide. Even more troublesome, those smooth curves going up, then down, turn out to be misleading. They are what you get when you plot data for poor and rich countries together at a given moment in time, but actual levels of various pollutants in any individual country plotted over time wiggle around a lot more. This suggests that the familiar bell-shaped curve reflects no immutable law, and that intelligent government policies might well help to reduce pollution levels even while countries are still relatively poor.

Local Antipollution Strategies

Developing countries are getting the message. From Mexico to the Philippines, they are now trying to curb the worst of the air and water pollution that typically accompanies industrialisation. China, for example, was persuaded by outside experts that it was losing so much potential economic output through health troubles caused by pollution (according to one World Bank study, somewhere between 3.5% and 7.7% of GDP [gross domestic product]) that tackling it was cheaper than ignoring it.

Local people usually have a better knowledge of local ecological conditions than experts . . . , as well as a direct interest in improving the quality of life in their village.

One powerful—and until recently ignored—weapon in the fight for a better environment is local people. Old-fashioned paternalists in the capitals of developing countries used to argue that poor villagers could not be relied on to look after natural resources. In fact, much academic research has shown that the poor are more often victims than perpetrators of resource depletion: it tends to be rich locals or outsiders who are responsible for the worst exploitation.

Local people usually have a better knowledge of local ecological conditions than experts in faraway capitals, as well as a direct interest in improving the quality of life in their village.

A good example of this comes from the bone-dry state of Rajasthan in India, where local activism and indigenous know-how about rainwater "harvesting" provided the people with reliable water supplies—something the government had failed to do. In Bangladesh, villages with active community groups or concerned mullahs [religious leaders] proved greener than less active neighbouring villages.

Community-based forestry initiatives from Bolivia to Nepal have shown that local people can be good custodians of nature. Several hundred million of the world's poorest people live in and around forests. Giving those villagers an incentive to preserve forests by allowing sustainable levels of harvesting, it turns out, is a far better way to save those forests than erecting tall fences around them.

To harness local energies effectively, it is particularly important to give local people secure property rights, argues Mr. Dasgupta. In most parts of the developing world, control over resources at the village level is ill-defined. This often means that local elites usurp a disproportionate share of those resources, and that individuals have little incentive to maintain and upgrade forests or agricultural land. Authorities in Thailand tried to remedy this problem by distributing 5.5m land titles over a 20-year period. Agricultural output increased, access to credit improved and the value of the land shot up.

Rich countries must do more than make pious noises about global threats to the environment.

A Role for Rich Countries

Another powerful tool for improving the local environment is the free flow of information. As local democracy flourishes, ordinary people are pressing for greater environmental disclosure by companies. In some countries, such as Indonesia, governments have adopted a "sunshine" policy that involves naming and shaming companies that do not meet environmental regulations. It seems to achieve results.

Bringing greenery to the grass roots is good, but on its own it will not avert perceived threats to global "public goods" such as the climate or biodiversity. Paul Portney of Resources for the Future explains: "Brazilian villagers may think very carefully and unselfishly about their future descendants, but there's no reason for them to care about and protect species or habitats that no future generation of Brazilians will care about."

That is why rich countries must do more than make pious noises about global threats to the environment. If they believe that scientific evidence suggests a credible threat, they must be willing to pay poor countries to protect such things as their tropical forests. Rather than thinking of this as charity, they should see it as payment for environmental services (say, for carbon storage) or as a form of insurance.

In the case of biodiversity, such payments could even be seen as a trade in luxury goods: rich countries would pay poor countries to look after creatures that only the rich care about. Indeed, private green groups are already buying up biodiversity "hot spots" to protect them. One such initiative, led by Conservation International and the International Union for the Conservation of Nature (IUCN), put the cost of buying and preserving 25 hot spots exceptionally rich in species diversity at less than $30 billion. Sceptics say it will cost more, as hot spots will need buffer zones of "sustainable harvesting" around them. Whatever the right figure, such creative approaches are more likely to achieve results than bullying the poor into conservation.

It is not that the poor do not have green concerns, but that those concerns are very different from those of the rich. In Beijing's Da Shilan, for instance, the air is full of soot from the many tiny coal boilers. Unlike most of the neighbouring districts, which have recently converted from coal to natural gas, this area has been considered too poor to make the transition. Yet ask Liu Shihua, a shopkeeper who has lived in the same spot for over 20 years, and he insists he would readily pay a bit more for the cleaner air that would come from using natural gas. So would his neighbours.

To discover the best reason why poor countries should not ignore pollution, ask those two little boys outside Mr Liu's shop what colour the sky is. "Grey!" says one tyke, as if it were the most obvious thing in the world. "No, stupid, it's blue!" retorts the other. The children deserve blue skies and clean air. And now there is reason to think they will see them in their lifetime.

The Global Water Crisis Disproportionately Affects the Developing World

Nicholas L. Cain and Peter H. Gleick

Nicholas L. Cain is director of communications and Peter H. Gleick is president of the Pacific Institute, an independent research and policy organization that focuses on sustainable development, environmental protection, and international security, located in Oakland, California.

People living in the United States or any industrialized nation take safe drinking water for granted. But in much of the developing world, access to clean water is not guaranteed. According to the World Health Organization, more than 1.2 billion people lack access to clean water, and more than 5 million people die every year from contaminated water or water-related diseases.

The world's nations, through the United Nations (UN), have recognized the critical importance of improving access to clean water and ensuring adequate sanitation and have pledged to cut the proportion of people without such access by half by 2015 as part of the UN Millennium Development Goals. However, even if these goals are reached, tens of millions of people will probably perish from tainted water and water-borne diseases by 2020.

A Reachable Goal

Although ensuring clean water for all is a daunting task, the good news is that the technological know-how exists to treat and clean water and convey it safely. The international aid

Nicholas L. Cain and Peter H. Gleick, "The Global Water Crisis," *Issues in Science and Technology*, vol. 21, no. 4, summer 2005, pp. 79–81. Copyright 2005 National Academy of Sciences. Reproduced by permission of the authors.

community and many at-risk nations are already working on a range of efforts to improve access to water and sanitation.

It is clear, however, that more aid will be needed, although the estimates of how much vary widely. There is also considerable debate about the proper mix of larger, more costly projects and smaller, more community-scale projects. Still, it seems that bringing basic water services to the world's poorest people could be done at a reasonable price probably far less than consumers in developed countries now spend on bottled water.

The Toll of the Water Crisis

The global water crisis is a serious threat, and not only to those who suffer, get sick, and die from tainted water or water-borne disease. There is also a growing realization that the water crisis undercuts economic growth in developing nations, can worsen conflicts over resources, and can even affect global security by worsening conditions in states that are close to failure.

According to a Pacific Institute analysis, between 34 and 76 million people could perish because of contaminated water or water-related diseases by 2020, even if the UN Millennium Development Goals are met.

Despite the toll of the global water crisis, industrial nations spend little on overseas development efforts such as water and sanitation projects. Only 5 of 22 nations have met the modest UN goal of spending 0.7 percent of a nation's gross national income on overseas development assistance. And only a fraction of all international assistance is spent on water and sanitation projects. From 1999 to 2001, an average of only $3 billion annually was provided for water supply and sanitation projects.

The Expense of Bottled Water

Although tap water, in most of the developed world is clean and safe, millions of consumers drink bottled water for taste, convenience, or because of worries about water quality. Comprehensive data on bottled water consumption in the developing world are scarce. However, some water experts are worried that increased sales of bottled water to the developing world will reduce pressure on governments to provide basic access to non-bottled water. Others are concerned that the world's poorest people will have to spend a significant amount of their already low incomes to purchase water.

Consumers spend nearly $100 billion annually on bottled water, according to Pacific Institute estimates. Indeed, consumers often pay several hundred to a thousand times as much for bottled water as they do for reliable, high-quality tap water, which costs $.50 per cubic meter in California. This disparity is often worse in developing nations where clean water is far out of reach for the poorest people.

Government Corruption Seriously Hinders Economic Progress in Developing Nations

Isabel Blackett

Isabel Blackett is the chief executive of the Australian office of Transparency International, an international organization dedicated to fighting corruption around the world.

We go about our daily lives without the need to bribe anyone to obtain services, justice or information. We are treated by the doctor, admittted to hospital, and our children are educated. We can obtain a driving licence, phone and electricity connections without having to consider making illegal payments. But in many countries developing or 'in transition', this is not the case. Aside from the moral dilemmas, personal cost and injustice of such a situation, corruption at the highest level of government can have further serious implications for the lives of ordinary people and development of the nation.

The Impact of Corruption

"All over the world countries that should be rich remain poor. Though blessed with valuable minerals such as oil, diamonds and gold, the ordinary people of Angola, Nigeria, Kazakhstan and elsewhere are mired in poverty while corrupt officials prosper. Money that could be used to reduce poverty and jump start growth is stolen instead." And likewise, when the limited incomes of the poorest nations are wasted or stolen because of corruption, the most basic services of water supply,

Isabel Blackett, "Corruption: Whose Problem Is It?" *Harambee*, vol. XI, no. 3, September 2002. www.tear.org.au/resources/harambee. Reproduced by permission of TEAR Australia, Inc.

sanitation, roads, education, health and transport are not available to the ordinary citizen. The trap of poverty is propagated and sustained by corruption.

During the mid 1990s, corruption rapidly changed from being unmentionable, to appearing on a range of agendas at international conferences.

In more specific terms, grand corruption [usually involving political leaders and large sums of money] leads to:

- *Over-priced contracts* due to lack of genuine competition.

- *Low quality construction and services* due to inappropriate contractors, the inability of the 'bought' officials to supervise properly, and the need to recover money spent in bribes, resulting in high maintenance or replacement costs.

- Companies operating on an *unethical basis*, leaving them open to further erosion of standards and potential blackmail.

- The possibility that the *contract should never have been undertaken* at all.

However, at a national level, grand corruption has far-reaching negative impacts, as it will:

- undermine both free and fair trade, which should be based on price, quality and service

- hinder national, international and multi-national companies from operating legally and ethically

- distort development priorities affecting equity and the distribution of resources and services, as decisions are based on benefits to officials rather than needs of the poor.

- and therefore hinder progress and economic development.

In 1999, the World Bank estimated that US$80 billion was given or received in bribes and 'pay offs' each year—equivalent to about 45 percent of the investment and aid that flows from the developed to the developing world each year. Transparency International estimates that this may even be less than the actual damage and wastage caused by corruption, as it calculates the bribes as a percentage of contract value. However, often the entire value of the contract may be wasted, because the wrong projects are undertaken.

The Emergence of "Transparency" as a Concept

During the mid 1990s, corruption rapidly changed from being unmentionable, to appearing on a range of agendas at international conferences, business and trade gatherings, development and academic conferences. The word 'transparency' began to appear for the first time.

The political imperatives of the Cold War had blinded many aid donors and business people to the motives and personal agendas of the leaders and elites in many nations. With the end of this era, the 1990s saw an increased openness and willingness to address governance issues, and to question the effectiveness of bi-lateral and multi-lateral aid. Democracy movements demanded that corruption be addressed. Corruption became a key election issue in many places across all continents.

While questions are asked about the World Bank's role in development and its less-than-perfect track record, the willingness of the [former] President, James Wolfensohn, to address corruption has had a notable and positive effect. The World Bank now states:

The Bank has identified corruption as the single greatest obstacle to economic and social development. It undermines development by distorting the rule of law and weakening the institutional foundation on which economic growth depends.

Sadly, the effects of grand corruption are largely borne by the poor in developing nations, while the spoils are shared by . . . local elites, domestic and foreign companies.

This new climate, change of attitude, and the emergence of Transparency International and others has put good governance and combating corruption firmly on the agenda.

The Debt Connector

Aside from debt caused by arms purchasing, military involvement, and disasters, a portion of the debt owed by developing nations has been spent on projects motivated by personal gain of the officials involved. This has resulted in further public debt, low quality construction, and overpriced projects. The call by Jubilee 2000 [an international coalition of forty countries calling for the canceling of debts of developing countries] for debt forgiveness recognises that corruption has partly caused the debt. Below [Professor] Joe Remenyi argues that denying debt relief on the basis of corrupt officials is punishing the wrong people:

> . . . Another source of debt accumulation is grand corruption and official misuse of borrowed resources. . . . No other area of how developing countries have gotten into debt is so emotively tackled in the debt reduction arena. . . . But there is an anomaly here! If debt relief is to be denied because some debt has found its way into bank accounts owned by dishonest political leaders, does this not punish the wrong people?
>
> The just and ethical response to gross corruption must be active restitution by the closure of such accounts and the re-

patriation of these amounts to the cause of debt reduction. By insisting on the repayment of ill-gotten sums held in developed country banks through the misappropriation of borrowed money, we are simply adding to the burden of the poor, who have had no say in it at all. . . . By continuing to hold these deposits, lender agencies become partners in grand corruption at the expense of the poor.

. . . the effects of corruption are largely borne by the poor in the developing nations, while the spoils are shared by sections of the local elites, domestic and foreign companies.

A common perception that corruption is 'over there' and is the problem of developing nations masks many truths. Sadly, the effects of grand corruption are largely borne by the poor in developing nations, while the spoils are shared by sections of the local elites, domestic and foreign companies. Within each country, the history of the civil service, rule of law, independence of the judiciary, freedom of the press, the nature of the democratic system, existence of independent 'watchdog' agencies and other factors affect the causes and level of corruption.

Western Tolerance of Corruption

For years many western businesses have operated in a dualistic way: at home corrupt practices are illegal and entirely taboo (although they still happen on occasion) but overseas are regarded as more or less acceptable. There are two main reasons for this.

Firstly, in all Organisation for Economic Cooperation and Development (OECD) countries (except the United States) it was legal, until 1998–9 (and a tax-deductible business expense) to give bribes in other countries. Although illegal in the country where the bribes were given, it was perceived that the risk of getting caught was low compared to the value of contracts. Still today the proceeds of corruption are largely invested within the western banking system, although overseas bribery is now a criminal offence in Australia and other OECD countries.

The second problem is more insidious. Many western businesses were led to believe, even publicly advised, that bribery and corruption was part of normal business:

> ... now when you're talking about kickbacks, you're talking about something that's illegal in this country, and that of course, you wouldn't dream of doing. In many countries in the world the only way in which money trickles down is from the head of the country who owns everything. Now that's not immoral, or corrupt. We must be very careful not to insist that our practices are followed everywhere in the world.

> I have bribed government ministers and officials of all grades, in the form of cash payments, commissions, introductory fees, new cars, hospital treatment and so on for more than 40 years. That is the way one does business in those places. . . .

This 'cultural argument' has been increasingly discredited now [that] people in many new democracies have a voice, denied under previous regimes. In March 2001 Slobodan Milosovic [former president of Serbia and Yugoslavia] was arrested on corruption and plunder charges by his own people in Serbia—not for his many alleged human rights atrocities against Bosnians. How can the 'cultural argument' stand up to the Indonesian public protests against former President [Abdurrahan] Wahid's alleged involvement in a financial scandal, and the public outrage in the Philippines over former President [Joseph] Estrada's plunder of national resources? The story of democracy making people more intolerant of corrupt leaders is repeated time and again, although democracy in itself is not enough to eliminate corruption.

As clearly corruption is common, even endemic in many nations, a more reasonable argument is that it is a convenient and profitable 'habit' for certain sections of the elite—not the culture of the country or the people. . . .

Corruption is a world-wide problem, dating back to Old Testament times or before. As globalisation becomes an increasing reality, international corruption becomes our problem too, more than ever before. Corruption will not be eliminated while humans live, but must be effectively curbed and restrained if nations are going to prosper and poverty be reduced.

Population Growth Could Overwhelm Many Already Struggling Developing Nations

Michael Bowman

Michael Bowman is a reporter for Voice of America, an international broadcasting service funded by the U.S. government that broadcasts news, information, educational, and cultural programming every week throughout the world.

By 2050, world population is projected to reach nine billion people. That would constitute a 38 percent jump from today's population total of 6.5 billion, and more than five times the 1.6 billion people believed to have existed in 1900. Demographers foresee declining, more aged populations in many industrialized nations, and explosively-growing, ever-younger populations in much of the developing world.... Both trends are seen as problematic.

Future Population Growth in Developing Countries

If projections hold true, future global population growth will be heavily concentrated in Latin America, Africa and South Asia. Carl Haub is senior demographer at the Washington [D.C.]–based Population Reference Bureau. "All world population growth today is in the developing world. There is no natural population growth in Europe, and even the U.S. is very heavily dependent on immigration," he said.

By 2050, Africa's population, both northern and sub-Saharan, is expected to surge from 900 million to almost two billion, while South Asia's population is projected to swell

Michael Bowman, "World Population Growth to Be Concentrated in Developing Nations, as Total Expected to Reach Nine Billion by 2050," *VOANews.com*, March 7, 2006. Reproduced by permission.

from 1.6 billion to nearly 2.5 billion. At the same time, Europe's population is expected to shrink from 730 million to 660 million.

Many developing nations are struggling to provide for their current populations, and could be overwhelmed by future demographic growth.

Haub has sobering words for African governments worried about resource management in the face of explosive population growth, or European governments concerned about providing for an increasingly aged population: in the short-term, little can be done. "Demographic momentum is such that you cannot change something overnight. We cannot go back and have the babies we should have had in 1985. Whatever goal you might set, you have to start doing something about it about a generation ahead of time," he said.

The bottom line is that fertility rates will likely remain low in regions where babies are most-wanted from a public policy standpoint, and highest in many regions where poverty and hunger are already prevalent. The United Nations Population Fund's Africa Director, Fama Hane Ba, says many developing nations are struggling to provide for their current populations, and could be overwhelmed by future demographic growth. "One of the consequences is the tremendous challenges to the countries, the governments and the populations to take care and to provide social services, to these growing populations, and also employment opportunities," she said.

Experts also foresee increased urbanization in the developing world. Elizabeth Chacko, who teaches geography and South Asia studies at George Washington University, comes from India, which is expected to account for one-fifth of world population growth over the next 50 years. "When you think about population growth at large, there is the density factor. People do not just spread evenly across the country. They are crowded in the cities, they are crowded in the coastal plains. And that makes for all kinds of problems. We know that with higher density there are often higher rates of crime, greater chance of the spread of epidemics," she said. But Chacko notes that population growth can also generate a larger workforce and a bigger consumer base, both of which tend to propel economic growth.

Strategies for Changing Birthrates

At the Washington [D.C.]–based American Enterprise Institute, demography expert Nicholas Eberstadt warns that 50 year population projections can prove inaccurate, since they involve predicting the reproductive habits of a generation that has yet to be born. Nevertheless, to the extent that rapid population growth is anticipated in the developing world, he says it need not spell disaster for the poor. "In low-income areas there is continuing population growth. Does that mean unemployable people, or does that mean a vibrant workforce? It depends an awful lot on the sorts of policies and institutional settings in which one finds oneself. That seems to me to be a good argument for getting policies right and institutions good, rather than trying to fine-tune the birthrate," he said.

Many developing nations have programs to promote contraception.

Eberstadt makes a similar argument for industrialized nations, noting that efforts by European governments to promote higher birthrates have met with little success. "Inducing women to become—let's call them 'baby ranchers'—is a very expensive proposition when women have alternative occupations in the paid labor force. Most Western European countries have tried to 'talk up' the birth rate, and not surprisingly that does not work too well," he said.

Chacko notes that many developing nations have programs to promote contraception. She says she sees a common thread in regions where those programs have proven most successful: the empowerment of women. "[The state of] Kerala in southern India has had one of the lowest fertility rates [in the country] and everything we know about Kerala suggests that the women in the state have a high status; they have been educated; they have been working for a long time. And research has shown that even a few years of education can have a great impact on fertility rates, because this is a woman who can read, who can understand the kind of birth control she might want to use—but also be empowered to use it," she said.

Among developed nations, the United States is an enigma. Unlike Europe, the U.S. population is expected to increase by one-third by 2050. Demographers note that the United States continues to receive large numbers of immigrants, predominantly from Latin America, and that immigrants tend to have higher birthrates than the domestic population as a whole. They also note that higher standards of living allow many American women to successfully rear children on their own, and that American men generally share child rearing duties to a larger extent than their counterparts in other nations.

CHAPTER 2

Will Globalization Help
Developing Nations?

Chapter Preface

The term "globalization" usually refers to the increasingly quick and easy movement of goods, services, money, people, and information around the world, but the heart of the globalization phenomenon is liberal global trade polices. Although countries and companies have been trading with each other for centuries, the end of the Cold War, recent advancements in communications and other technologies, and the promotion of pro-trade policies by many developed countries have led to much more rapid growth of the phenomenon known as globalization.

Efforts by the developed world to help poorer countries build their economies through trade began decades ago in the aftermath of World War II. In July 1944, leading economists, politicians, bankers, and corporate leaders from around the world met at Bretton Woods, New Hampshire, to discuss ways to repair the devastation caused by the war. Agreements were signed at this meeting to create the World Bank and the International Monetary Fund (IMF), two institutions that since that time have provided loans and other assistance to countries in need of economic development.

The push for creating a global trading system began just a few years later, in 1947, when twenty-three countries signed the General Agreement on Tariffs and Trade (GATT), a treaty to promote global trade. Over the next few decades, trade talks among GATT countries produced a series of trade concessions, many of which involved lowering or removing national tariffs, taxes, and subsidies for various types of goods and services traded between countries. Enacting these trade concessions made it easier and more profitable for nations to trade with each other. Other changes in monetary policies made it feasible for banks and corporations to move money to and from worldwide operations more quickly. Still other changes, such as the expansion of intellectual property rights—that is, legal protections for writings (copyright), inventions (patents), manufacturing processes (trade secrets), and product identifiers (trademarks)—further encouraged global trade.

The collapse of the Soviet Union in 1991, which ended the Cold War tensions between capitalist and Communist nations, also helped to pave the way for an expansion of world trade. A final GATT meeting in 1994 created the World Trade Organization (WTO) an international institution to promote liberal global trade, and established GATT as the economic law of the world. Under this global trade system, corporations are permitted to challenge governmental regulations and laws that are believed to be barriers to global trade. Also in the 1990s, several free-trade agreements were negotiated between certain individual countries to expand trading opportunities even further among treaty signatories. One of these agreements was the North American Free Trade Agreement (NAFTA), which provides for enhanced trade among Mexico, the United States, and Canada.

Beginning in the late 1990s, however, the movement toward global trade suffered several setbacks that slowed its progress. In 1997, a financial crisis occurred in Asia, a region that had been experiencing strong economic growth. South Korea, Indonesia, and Thailand were hit hardest, but the effects of the crisis also rippled across the globe, causing investors to lose confidence in emerging markets of many developing nations. Although the cause of the crisis was a controversial topic, many experts blamed it on loosened monetary rules that allowed investors to pull funds out of the area very quickly, and other free-trade policies pushed by the WTO and IMF.

In 1999, globalization suffered another blow when large-scale public protests erupted against globalization in Seattle, Washington, during WTO trade talks. Demonstrations also disrupted WTO and IMF meetings in Washington, D.C., in the spring of 2000. Protesters charged that globalization is orchestrated and dominated by a handful of U.S. and Western multinational corporations that seek profits for shareholders at the expense of local and national concerns in many developing countries. Although globalization supporters believe global trade offers the best opportunity for poor countries to develop their economies, critics charge that globalization policies have brought only greater poverty and economic volatility to many developing nations.

One concern of critics, for example, involves what they view as unfair trade rules. Under global trade policies promoted by the WTO and IMF, for example, many developing countries were encouraged to eliminate protections for their products and tariffs on imported goods, and to open their economies to foreign investment and global trade, while highly developed countries such as the United States and Great Britain continued to maintain subsidies and trade barriers to protect some of their industries from global competition. One of the most glaring inequities involved developing countries' protections of their agricultural products—a highly sought-after market for many developing countries such as those in Africa, which have rural, farm-based economies.

The criticisms of globalization led to a new series of trade talks launched at Doha, Qatar, in 2001 designed to aid the world's poor and promote fairer trade with developing countries. The goals of the Doha trade negotiations included correcting the inequities of previous trade agreements, giving developing nations more flexibility in developing their economies, and eliminating agricultural subsidies in the developed countries.

The Doha talks, however, have failed to reach these goals. Talks collapsed at a 2003 summit in Cancún, Mexico, when developing countries became frustrated with a lack of progress in negotiations over rich countries' agricultural subsidies and other development issues. A 2005 meeting in Hong Kong suffered a similar deadlock in negotiations, and the Doha round of talks completely collapsed at a July 2006 meeting in Geneva, Switzerland. Largely as a result of continuing disagreements about farm subsidies and tariffs, the Doha effort has been indefinitely suspended by the WTO.

The authors of the selections in this chapter discuss the issue of whether globalization has helped or hurt developing countries, and provide more information about the impact of international trade rules.

Global Trade Has Brought Economic Growth to Developing Countries

John L. Manzella

John L. Manzella is a trade consultant and the author of the book Grasping Globalization: Its Impact and Your Corporate Response *(2005).*

The answer to the question, "has globalization harmed developing countries?" is "No!" Quite the contrary, in fact. Trade and globalization have improved the lives of billions of people in developing countries. For example, in the short span of 1990 through 1998, the number of people living in extreme poverty in East Asia and the Pacific decreased 41 percent—one of the largest and most rapid reductions in history.

Today, 24 developing countries representing about 3 billion people, including China, India and Mexico, have adopted policies enabling their citizens to take advantage of globalization. The net result is that their economies are catching up with rich ones. Over the last two decades, according to the World Bank, these 24 countries achieved higher growth in incomes, longer life expectancy and better schooling. The incomes of the least globalized countries during this same period, including Iran, Pakistan and North Korea, dropped or remained static. What distinguishes the fastest growing developing countries from the slowest is clear: their openness to trade.

Global Trade and Poverty

For many of the world's poorest countries, the primary problem is not too much globalization, but their inability to participate in it. Study after study corroborate this. For example,

John L. Manzella, "Have Trade and Globalization Harmed Developing Countries?" *World Trade*, vol. 19, no. 1, January 2006, p. 8. Copyright © 2006 BNP Media. Reproduced by permission.

the WTO [World Trade Organization] report, *Trade, Income Disparity and Poverty*, says, "Trade liberalization helps poor countries catch up with rich ones," and concludes that trade liberalization "is essential if poor people are to have any hope of a brighter future." *Globalization, Poverty and Inequality*, published by the Progressive Policy Institute, contends that less globalization is generally associated with less development, and concludes that no country has managed to lift itself out of poverty without integrating into the global economy.

And who would know this better than former Mexican President Ernesto Zedillo, who said, "In every case where a poor nation has significantly overcome its poverty, this has been achieved while engaging in production for export markets and opening itself to the influx of foreign goods, investment and technology—that is, by participating in globalization." Even former sociologist Fernando Henrique Cardoso, who spoke out against aspects of global dependence, promoted—not resisted—globalization as president of Brazil.

Developing countries with open economies grew by 4.5 percent a year in the 1970s and 1980s, while those with closed economies grew by 0.7 percent a year, concludes the National Bureau of Economic Research report *Economic Convergence and Economic Policies*. At this rate, open economies double in size every 16 years, while closed economies double every 100 years.

Globalization may not be a panacea for all economic ills, but it certainly helps alleviate them. However, it has had negative consequences on some developing countries with distorted economies or a lack of sound legal or financial systems. As a result, anti-globalists with good intentions but bad policy recommendations often make globalization the scapegoat for many of the world's problems.

In the end, the facts don't lie. Since the 1970s—when policies supporting globalization got traction—through 2001, world infant mortality rates decreased by almost half, adult literacy increased more than a third, primary school enrollment rose and the average life span shot up 11 years. Looking forward, from 2002 through 2025, life expectancy is projected to rise from 62 years to 68 years in less developed countries, the U.S. Census Bureau estimates.

Expanded Trade Necessary

The World Bank report *Globalization, Growth and Poverty: Building an Inclusive World Economy* suggests that globalization must be better harnessed to help the world's poorest, most marginalized countries improve the lives of their citizens—an especially important effort in the wake of September 11 [2001]. Agreed. But how to achieve this is not yet known.

In the meantime consider this. If remaining world merchandise trade barriers are eliminated, potential gains are estimated at $250 to $650 billion annually, according to the International Monetary Fund and World Bank. About one-third to one-half of these gains would accrue in developing countries. Removal of agricultural supports would raise global economic welfare by an additional $128 billion annually, with some $30 billion going to developing countries.

Freer Global Trade Could Eradicate Poverty and World Hunger

John Nash and Donald Mitchell

John Nash is an adviser for commodities and trade in the World Bank's Rural Development Department, and Donald Mitchell is lead economist in the Bank's Development Prospects Group.

Trade policy may not, at first glance, seem like the ideal tool for combating hunger. But eradicating costly protectionist barriers may be one of the best ways to put food on the tables of the poor. The world produces more than enough food to feed everyone. Yet about 840 million people, or almost one-sixth of the world's population, still suffer from undernourishment. The overwhelming majority of these—about 92 percent—suffer from chronic undernutrition, rather than the acute hunger that grabs headlines in periods of man-made or natural disasters.

Part of the problem is the obsession in both developed and developing countries with the idea that increasing national food crop production, rather than raising incomes, is the best way to achieve food security. This preoccupation in developing countries has been exacerbated by the inordinately high support for agricultural production in industrialized countries, which causes huge distortions in global food markets. It has been a costly distraction both in countries' own policies and in negotiations in the World Trade Organization's (WTO) Doha Round trade talks [a series of global negotiations on trade and development].

John Nash and Donald Mitchell, "How Freer Trade Can Help Feed the Poor: An Agenda for Easing Hunger Worldwide by Reducing Trade Protectionism," *Finance & Development*, vol. 42, no. 1, March 2005, pp. 34–37. Copyright © 2005 International Monetary Fund. Republished with permission of International Monetary Fund, conveyed through Copyright Clearance Center, Inc.

Global trade liberalization is only one weapon in the arsenal to fight hunger, but it can make an important contribution by delivering cheaper food in protectionist countries and boosting the global economy, helping to lift millions out of poverty. This is one reason why it is essential that the Doha Round agreement lower barriers to trade in food products in rich and poor countries. This article examines how trade policy can be harnessed to help reduce poverty and alleviate hunger and outlines an agenda to reduce food insecurity in developing countries.

Production Increases and Protectionism

Food production, stocks, and exporting capacity are not at the root of the problem of undernutrition. Grain prices have been falling over the past 25 years thanks to global surpluses. Despite a reduction in global cropland used for grain production, particularly in the five largest exporting areas—the United States, the European Union (EU), Canada, Australia, and Argentina—real prices for wheat have fallen by about 34 percent and for rice by almost 60 percent. The 2004/05 crop year [was] expected to see world grain production increase by 8 percent, the biggest year-on-year increase in 26 years, as a result of higher yields and better growing conditions in regions plagued by several years of drought. With consumption projected to increase by only 2 percent, the boost in production should lead to higher grain stocks.

In spite of adequate global supplies, and in part thanks to relatively low world prices, many countries impose import tariffs on food to encourage and protect higher-cost domestic production. While this is true of both industrialized and developing countries, the latter bear the brunt of much of the cost of both their own protectionist policies and those of the richer countries. Food protectionism results in higher domestic food prices, which mostly hurt poor consumers as they spend disproportionately on food. Protectionism does not benefit the rural poor equally as it leaves out two large groups: those who do not own farmland, but have to pay higher prices as consumers; and those who own farmland, but do not produce for commercial purposes. And even commercial farmers, who may see a short-term increase in their income, will not experience long-term benefits such as a significant narrowing of the income gap with nonfarmers; this will come only from measures that raise agricultural productivity and facilitate the movement of labor.

Policymakers often view protectionism as a substitute for more productive methods in support of agriculture, such as increased spending on rural education, infrastructure, research, and technical assistance. It keeps them from investing in efficient food distribution systems that would improve their ability to respond quickly to food emergencies. Simulations have shown that replacing the implicit tax on consumption that results from protectionism with an equivalent explicit tax and investing the revenue in agricultural research can be enormously beneficial for increasing employment, income, and consumption, particularly of food.

The real question is how the poor can be provided with ... sufficient income so they can meet their [food] consumption needs.

Protectionism also indirectly encourages farmers to continue planting low-value food crops instead of diversifying into high-value nontraditional exports that would be a better way of raising income and escaping poverty. In turn, the lack of export production reduces the country's ability to earn foreign exchange and undermines its structural capacity to import food and other products. And when many developing countries protect their food crops by imposing import tariffs, they are effectively creating high barriers to South-South trade. Thus, although there is a case to be made for temporary limited safeguard measures for developing countries with low import tariffs, in general, trade barriers on food make poor consumers less food secure, and even the temporary benefits to producers are debased in the longer run as the protectionism undermines more productive use of public and private investment resources and provokes reactive protection in other countries.

Apart from chronic food insecurity, there is a legitimate concern over temporary food supply disruptions caused by man-made or natural disasters, and this is sometimes used to justify protectionist measures to stimulate domestic food production. However, the impact of these disruptions could be mitigated through other measures, such as stockpiling of moderate reserves in cash or in kind, improving distribution channels, and reforming food aid, which would be more effective and less costly than efforts to stimulate food production. To the extent that disruptions stem from exporting countries restraining exports in times of high world prices, developing countries should act through the WTO to seek to constrain such behavior in the Doha agreement.

Focus on Raising Income

Because chronic food insecurity comes mainly from insufficient purchasing power of the poor, the real question is how the poor can be provided with opportunities to earn sufficient income so they can meet their consumption needs, regardless of whether they do so through food produced at home or abroad. Here, trade liberalization can have a major impact, as it would open markets for producers in developing countries not only to sell their products at higher prices, but also to buy better production technology, which in turn would help boost their productivity and raise their incomes. But this requires strong commitment from developing and industrialized countries to sweeping liberalization in the Doha trade negotiations. A successful Doha Round could produce huge benefits for the developing world and lift millions out of poverty. However, in the Doha talks, discussions of food security continue to center on domestic production, which is reflected in negotiating positions calling for more flexibility for developing countries—of some subset such as net food importing countries—to be exempted from the general obligations, so they can maintain high import barriers to food products under the rubric of "special products" or as a component of the "development box."

The focus on domestic production may be a holdover from the past, when the global food distribution system was less developed, food imports were primarily the responsibility of often inefficient state enterprises, and poor macroeconomic policies created the specter of foreign exchange shortages at times when food imports were most needed. But under current conditions, the strategy should aim at reducing poverty, not increasing domestic food production. While a comprehensive strategy to fight hunger needs to have many components, including nutritional education, health infrastructure, safety nets, and more, the main determinant of undernutrition is income. Whereas it is difficult to find an example of a country where large numbers of people were lifted out of poverty but are still going hungry because of a lack of locally produced food, there are prominent cases of countries that are food self-sufficient at a national level—even holding large surplus stock—but where large numbers of poor people continue to go hungry.

How Trade Liberalization Can Help

Clearly, when considering food security, the Doha trade liberalization talks need to shift the focus from how the trading system can be used to increase the degree of self-sufficiency to how it can help raise the incomes of the poor. In addition, to take advantage of the historic opportunity presented by the Round, the level of ambition in the negotiations needs to be ratcheted up. Developing countries can also take some unilateral steps that do not depend on the Round. The agenda should focus on these components, in rough order of priority:

- In a Doha Round agreement, all countries—rich and developing—should commit to lowering bound (ceiling) rates on food and other agricultural products to significantly reduce applied tariffs. This should be combined with a special safeguard or contingent protection mechanism for developing countries, which they can invoke in periods of exceptionally low world prices or import surges.

- Individual developing countries should enhance household food security by lowering applied tariffs on food product imports. To mitigate adverse effects on small producers who have limited resources to adjust, safety nets or transitional assistance schemes may be needed. While in principle such reforms are desirable even in the absence of multilateral negotiations, in practice they will be politically much easier if a successful agreement exists that calls for industrialized countries to reduce their own subsidies and border protection.

- Rural development strategies should focus policy, as well as productivity-enhancing investments and support services, on raising rural incomes and improving the environment for agricultural production in general (including exports), not on increasing food production. In many developing countries, agricultural investment needs to be increased, but in a way that creates a level playing field in which farmers can make unbiased production decisions.

- The practice of export taxation or controls by food-exporting countries in periods of high world prices should be restricted under the Doha Round agreement.

- Rich countries' dumping of surplus production, billed as food aid, in developing countries in periods of global gluts should also be disciplined in the agreement, as it undermines local food production and marketing channels.

- Developing countries should unilaterally lower regulatory and border barriers to trade in agricultural inputs such as seeds, fertilizers, chemicals, and equipment.

- Independently of the Doha Round, developing countries should lower barriers to cross-border regional trade in food products and invest in reducing the costs of this trade. Since shocks to the food supply are not perfectly correlated across neighboring countries, regional trade flows can help stabilize supplies and prices.

- Sweeping global trade liberalization could lead to a structural increase in global food prices, which could negatively impact poor consumers. However, there should be ample time for adjustment, as structural effects will appear gradually as agreements are implemented. In countries that currently impose tariffs on food imports, the domestic effect of higher world market prices can be offset by lowering tariffs. In other countries, safety nets may be needed to protect the most vulnerable. In addition, world prices will become less volatile, helping producers and consumers manage risks better. Nevertheless, a WTO panel is currently exploring ways to help poor consumers deal with potentially higher prices.

The international trading system can clearly play a role in alleviating hunger, but governments and negotiators need to look beyond the short-term effects of protectionist barriers and work toward an open system that allows all people physical and economic access to sufficient, safe, and nutritious food.

A Case for Safeguarding Food Production

Although part of the solution to food security is to eradicate import barriers, in periods of exceptionally low world prices, developing countries that agree to significantly lower WTO-bound tariffs should be allowed to invoke special temporary measures to protect production. While rich countries protect their producers from the high volatility in agricultural markets through safety nets of various kinds, the poorer countries cannot afford to do so. Thus, developing countries will be looking for other ways to protect producers of import-substitute crops.

Ideally, this should be done by direct payments not linked to how much input is used or how much output is produced, rather than an increase in import tariffs. But taking into consideration fiscal realities, it is likely that protection would have to come from tariffs. However, any tariff increases under this special mechanism should be time-bound, moderate in magnitude, and invoked only on rare occasions. Such constraints will at least minimize the inherent bias against exports that is created by protection. And this relatively neutral trade policy with no or modest protection for import substitutes would not hurt food production. In many countries, farmers traditionally follow a mixed-crop strategy, and the production of cash crops improves their ability to buy modern components for their food production. Hence, a positive empirical correlation exists between cash crop income and food production. This relationship is stronger in poorer countries, where non-farm income is more limited.

Globalization Provides Opportunities for Young People in Developing Nations

Population Briefs

Population Briefs is a research newsletter published three times a year by the Population Council, an international nonprofit nongovernmental organization that conducts biomedical, social science, and public health research.

The largest-ever generation of people aged 10–24 is now making the transition from childhood to adulthood. One and a half billion of them—66 percent—live in developing countries. Adolescence is a pivotal stage of physical, emotional, cognitive, social, and economic transitions, often characterized—particularly for girls—by lack of autonomy. The nature and quality of young people's adult lives, as well as a country's social and economic development, depend on how successfully they navigate this critical period.

[In 2002], the U.S. National Academies [a society of distinguished scholars that advises the government on matters of science and technology] asked Cynthia B. Lloyd, Population Council director of social science research, to lead an expert panel in examining transitions to adulthood in developing countries and outlining the policy implications of its findings. Two other Council senior social scientists, Shireen Jejeebhoy and Barbara Mensch, also participated on the 15-member panel, which focused particularly on the influence of gender. Population Council researchers have concentrated on the study of adolescents since the early 1990s, committed to moving the field of adolescent policy research from a narrow focus on sexuality and reproductive health to broader attention to social and economic issues that underpin adolescent health.

Population Briefs, "Globalization Is Transforming Adolescence in the Developing World," vol. 11, no. 2, May 2005, pp. 1–2. Copyright © 2005 The Population Council, Inc. Reproduced by permission.

In 2005, the panel's investigations culminated in the publication of *Growing Up Global: The Changing Transitions to Adulthood in Developing Countries*. The panel found that despite widespread progress in certain areas, many young people still lack good health and adequate schooling—both of which are essential for ensuring their productivity and well-being. The lives of many of these young men and women are profoundly different from those of their parents. While change itself is not new, the speed of globalization has accelerated and its scale has widened.

Health

Growing Up Global reports that, on average, this generation is healthier and has an improved chance of surviving to old age, compared to the same age group 20 years ago. But HIV/AIDS has had a hugely negative impact on young people, most notably in sub-Saharan Africa, where the disease is now the leading cause of death for 15–29-year-olds. More young women than young men die of AIDS in that region. "Young women, particularly the youngest adolescent girls, also face increased risk of death and disease related to first pregnancy, childbirth, and unsafe abortion," elaborates Jejeebhoy. The panel concluded that unprotected sex is one of the riskiest behaviors that young people can undertake. Simultaneously, tobacco use is increasing throughout the developing world, and the gender gap in smoking prevalence is rapidly closing, with more young women taking up the practice. There is also evidence that illicit drug use among young people is rising, and alcohol use is expected to go up.

Schooling

The panel's review of educational trends provides a revealing indication of the future because school is the most influential transforming agent in society, after the family. The numbers show that young people in the developing world are now more likely than in the past to attend school during adolescence and postpone entering the labor force. But there remain large differences in school attendance rates according to wealth and residential status, with poor girls suffering particular disadvantage.

Rising school enrollment, trends toward greater democratization, greater access to the media, and globalization have all increased opportunities for young people.

Although global trends in population, health, urbanization, and education have contributed positively to the demand for education, many schools are of poor quality, thus limiting enrollment, encouraging dropout, and compromising learning. "Results from recent internationally comparable standardized tests raise serious concerns about how much students are actually learning," says Lloyd.

Nevertheless, the economic payoff for attending high school and college is consistently high, and the gap in income, job stability, and upward mobility between those who have attended only primary school and those who have completed more schooling is widening. In many parts of Asia, Latin America, and the Caribbean, increasing numbers of young people have been absorbed into the labor force without any large rise in youth unemployment; yet the challenge of providing employment for young people remains substantial in some of the poorer countries of Asia, sub-Saharan Africa, and the Middle East, given unprecedented growth in younger populations.

Rising school enrollment, trends toward greater democratization, greater access to the media, and globalization have all increased opportunities for young people to become active and involved members of their communities. Although television, radio, and newspapers are becoming more accessible to young people, their availability varies greatly by region. Among

15–19-year-olds, for example, 22 percent in southern and east-ern Africa watch television at least once a week, compared with 91 percent in former Soviet Asia. The media, along with schools, employers, national service programs, and sports and other informal youth programs, play increasingly important roles in citizenship formation.

Early Marriage

Marriage prior to age 18 is considered by many to be a hu-man rights violation. According to Demographic and Health Survey data, which cover 60 percent of the developing world's population, nearly 40 percent of young women marry before that age—down from about 50 percent two decades ago. Al-though the fraction of girls who marry at a young age is still substantial, Mensch observes that "the decline in early mar-riage is quite widespread, lending support to the notion that global changes are affecting the transition to adulthood." How-ever, even marked improvement in some areas is insufficient to fully overcome certain inequities. Young women in the de-veloping world who marry as minors are more likely to come from poor households and rural areas and to have relatively little schooling.

Poverty is the greatest barrier to making a successful transition to adulthood.

Entry into marriage is strongly associated with entry into parenthood. More than 90 percent of first births occur within marriage, and this percentage has changed only minimally over the past 20 years. Early childbearing remains common in many parts of the developing world because of high rates of early marriage. According to Demographic and Health Survey data, 23 percent of young women aged 20–24 in the develop-ing world gave birth before age 18. By comparison, in the

United States in 1995, only 9 percent of young women aged 20–24 gave birth before age 18.

Poverty is the greatest barrier to making a successful transition to adulthood. As a percentage of the population, poverty rates have declined worldwide, except in sub-Saharan Africa. But as a result of rapid population growth, the number of young people living in poor families is roughly the same as it was ten years ago—825 million. There are more young people surviving on one dollar a day than there are people living in the United States, where the current population is roughly 300 million.

Policy Recommendations

Substantial investments in the health and schooling of young people will equip them to participate constructively in shaping their own and their countries' future. Policies and programs, if they are to be effective, must be evidence-based, locally appropriate, and designed in cooperation with developing-country governments and local communities.

Policies and programs designed to enhance successful transitions for young people should be targeted to the poor, particularly poor young women, who are often doubly disadvantaged. The panel also calls for interventions that promote gender equity in the arenas of citizenship, work, marriage, and parenthood in all social classes. "Achieving the United Nations Millennium Development Goals of universal primary schooling and gender equity in schooling will not be enough to ensure that the next generation of young people acquires the skills necessary for successful adulthood," says Lloyd. "Policymakers should give equal attention to school quality and expanding enrollments at the secondary level."

The panel recommends that policymakers increase the provision of general health information and sex education, including negotiating skills, for all young people and increase the availability of reproductive health services. Some of the most important reproductive health interventions for young people may lie outside the health sector. For example, school participation and higher levels of educational attainment appear to have positive associations with young people's health; both male and female students who remain enrolled during their teens are substantially less likely to have had sex than their unmarried peers who are not enrolled. Indeed, the growing percentage of adolescents attending school may have contributed to delays in the age of sexual initiation in some countries, which were documented by the panel. Thus, resources spent on expanding opportunities for secondary schooling may have a direct effect on the reproductive health of young people.

The challenges of promoting a successful passage to adulthood for young people in developing countries are significant. Investing in their health and schooling as well as in opportunities for productive livelihoods will greatly enhance young people's future prospects.

Global Trade Is Unfair for Developing Countries Because of Agricultural Trade Barriers

Moin Siddiqi

Moin Siddiqi is an economist and journalist who reports on economic issues affecting the Middle East, Africa, and Central Asia.

The Doha Development Agenda—the ninth round of global free trade talks launched in November 2001 by the World Trade Organisation (WTO) in the wake of the 9/11 [2001] terrorist outrage—presented what was described as an 'unparalleled opportunity' for all countries to reap benefits from a freer, fairer, multilateral trading system.

After five long years, the agenda has been exhausted and talks finally reached a stalemate. As India's trade minister Kamal Nath said: "The Doha round is definitely between intensive care and the crematorium." This failure dashes any hopes of making globalisation more inclusive and helping African farmers and manufacturers, particularly by tackling the problems of trade barriers and subsidies in farming, the rich world's most highly-protected industry.

It is a bitter irony that the 'quad' countries (Canada, the EU [European Union], Japan and US) spend six times as much on farm subsidies as the total world official-development aid budget. Big, wealthy farmers receive a disproportionately large share of government support in the US and EU since payments are based on area of land planted. The larger the area planted, the larger the government's support.

Moin Siddiqi, "Crunch Time for World Trade Deal: Once Again the Developing Countries Have Failed to Convince the Rich Nations to Play Fair in World Trade," *African Business*, vol. 324, October 2006, pp. 32–33. Copyright © IC Publication Ltd. Reproduced by permission.

The WTO talks originally set 1 January 2005 as the deadline for an ambitious Doha Treaty, the deadline subsequently revised to end [in] December 2006. The Doha Treaty was supposed to open up agricultural markets in rich countries and markets for industrial goods and services from prime developing nations (notably Brazil, China, India and South Africa).

A positive outcome to the Doha [talks] . . . would have lifted millions out of poverty.

The World Bank estimated that a positive outcome to the Doha round (i.e. the extra trade an agreement would generate) would mean gains in real income for all countries of about $100bn [billion] by 2015, with one-fifth accruing to developing countries. That would have lifted millions out of poverty. Advocates of free trade say a workable deal would fuel world growth and boost jobs, but there was an underlying fear that trade liberalisation would initially cost jobs in developing countries as infant industries became exposed to fierce competition from multinational companies.

Disappointing Outcome

Pascal Lamy, WTO director-general, urged the 149 member-countries to 'act decisively and with real urgency' to create a freer and fairer global trading system. However little, if any, tangible progress was achieved on three principal topics on the Doha agenda: slashing 'trade-distorting' tariffs and farm subsidies; moving forward with liberalisation of the trade in manufactur[ing] and deregulating service sectors (namely public utilities, financials and telecoms) in big emerging markets.

The December 2005 Hong Kong summit yielded only minimal results. The 'quad' countries agreed to phase out, by 2013, agricultural export subsidies—without a commitment on import tariffs. Empirical research and analysis shows that import tariffs are, in fact, more detrimental to poor nations than farm subsidies. Removal of export subsidies would harm food-importers by raising the price of subsidised products.

Regarding cotton production, the US and EU pledged to abolish export subsidies, but the US refused to set a timetable for reducing payments it made to its own growers. A decade ago, the US spent almost $10bn a year in subsidising its fortunate farmers; today it spends twice that amount. Cotton subsidies raise producer prices by over one-half in the US and even higher in the EU. India's trade minister put it succinctly: "Indian farmers can compete with US farmers but not with the US Treasury." Extensive subsidies allow US growers to export cotton at just one-third of actual production cost.

Trade restrictions prevent prosperity in non-fuel-exporting African countries that suffer from continuing unfavourable terms-of-trade for their main products.

Finally, the OECD [Organisation for Economic Co-operation and Development] countries offered the 32 least-developed countries (LDCs) quota-free, duty-free market access for 97% of their goods. Yet even this proposal was trimmed as textiles and sugar—where poorer WTO members enjoy a competitive edge thanks to cheaper labour costs— were excluded from the US's commitment, and Japan insisted on blocking rice imports.

The African Perspective

So far, mega trade rounds have offered hardly any commercial benefits for the continent, which accounts for just 3% of global trade. [Former] British Prime Minister Tony Blair pointed out that "a 1% increase in Africa's share of world trade will benefit Africa by over $70bn". The stumbling block remains free trade in agriculture, which accounts for 30% and 40%, respectively, of sub-Saharan Africa's GDP [gross domestic product, referring to a country's output of goods and services] and total exports, as well as providing the main source of income for 70% of the continent's population. Trade restrictions prevent prosperity in non-fuel-exporting African countries that suffer from continuing unfavourable terms-of-trade for their main products.

The EU's offer to end export subsidies by 2013, in fact, represents just 5.4% of total agricultural support, or 3bn [euros] compared to the 55bn [euros] it pays in domestic farm subsidies. Commenting on Europe's Common Agricultural Policy, [the relief agency] Oxfam notes: "EU consumers and taxpayers pay a high price for excessive production, but the real burden falls far beyond Europe's borders. Not only is Europe depressing the world price and keeping out efficient suppliers like Brazil and Thailand, it is also depressing prospects for some LDCs, such as Mozambique."

[Since the deadlock in Doha talks,] the major trading powers are moving to establish regional or bilateral trade deals with their strategic allies.

Likewise, the US's pledge to end cotton export subsidies covers just one-tenth of total government funding for the sector. Generous domestic payments to farmers underpin a global glut. A 2004 study by the UK's [United Kingdom] Overseas Development Institute found that removing the US's $4bn cotton subsidies would boost world prices by 20% or more. The main sub-Saharan African beneficiaries would be Benin, Burkina Faso, Chad, Mali and Togo.

Other research shows that West African cotton exports would increase by a massive 75% and the developing nations' share of global cotton exports would rise from 56% to 85% by 2015, if the West's domestic support programmes were abolished. Market access would also improve if excess tariffs in high-income countries were cut aggressively.

The US and EU have not discussed 'tariff peaks' imposed on chocolate bars from Ghana or other products where African countries generally enjoy a competitive advantage, such as textiles, garments, leather goods, furniture and footwear. These all attract heavy tariffs of 15% or higher which in turn deters foreign direct investment and the growth of Africa's manufacturing sector. Furthermore, these trade tariffs undermine export-diversification.

Potential Repercussions

The impact upon the global economy of a lengthy deadlock could prove far-reaching. The major trading powers are moving to establish regional or bilateral trade deals with their strategic allies. The US has negotiated free trade accords with 13 countries and is currently negotiating with 10 more—including Bahrain, Morocco, South Africa and Thailand. The EU is also expanding economic partnership agreements with the 69 African, Caribbean and Pacific countries group, all of which were former colonies.

According to [the] WTO secretariat, there are already 200 regional and bilateral trade agreements worldwide. But smaller economies have 'unequal' bargaining power in dealing with Brussels [Belgium] and Washington. Hans Peter Lankes, chief of the IMF's [International Monetary Fund] Trade Policy Division, said: "The breakdown [of global trade talks] weakens multilateralism. It will trigger an even more pronounced shift toward bilateral deals. The results, even with well-designed free trade agreements—and most aren't—are diminishing transparency, mounting trade discrimination and increasing red tape that will hamper cross-border production chains." The Confederation of British Industries agreed, stating: "Irretrievable failure would also entail substantial losses for business globally. Rapidly emerging economies, notably Brazil, India and South Africa, could keep exorbitantly high tariffs on a range of key imports and severe restrictions on services providers. Non-tariff barriers, those complex behind-the-border obstacles, would stay untouched."

At worst, protectionist pressures could increase if the global economy slows down in 2007/08. UK's *The Times* newspaper warns: "If the WTO is to regain its authority, it must control any resurgence of bilateral deals, which undermine the principle that all countries must be treated equally. If this cornerstone of trade rules is broken, the world would break up into the sort of blocs that helped to deepen worldwide recession in the 1930s."

On a more positive note, the developing world is working together more closely than ever before—cementing strong alliances between the Group-90 nations [a coalition of African, Caribbean, Pacific, and other less-developed areas] and large emerging markets. Brazil, India, and South Africa are aiming to create a free trade zone that would eventually increase trade among their respective continents. [From 2004 to 2006], Brazil's trade with India has sky-rocketed by 170%, while its trade with South Africa has surged 86%. If a formal alliance is agreed, future potentials are immense. Celso Amorim, Brazil's foreign minister, says: "With a trilateral treaty, trade would multiply. It isn't unthinkable to dream of $14bn to $15bn in a few years' time." Brazil would like Mercosur [South America's trade bloc] to expand its trade agreements to include India and South Africa.

The Way Forward

A concrete trade deal is achievable only if all parties stand to gain from it. This requires political compromises in Brussels and Washington on contentious issues such as farm subsidies and what is termed 'substantial market access' for processed agricultural products from developing countries. The latter should allow tariff reductions for manufactured goods and gradually open up services industries, in stages, to inward investments. The Doha round may not fail completely even if the end-2006 deadline is missed as previous rounds have taken many years to come to fruition.

Free Trade Alone Is Not a Panacea for Developing Countries

Sebastian Mallaby

Sebastian Mallaby is a columnist for the Washington Post *newspaper.*

[In 2000,] free-traders had a lazy time: Anti-globalization protesters were crude, their arguments easily deflated. Today a harder debate is underway. Troubling questions about trade are being raised by globalization's defenders. The risk is that politicians will seize hold of those questions and provide the wrong answers.

Free Trade Effects on Poor Nations

The first question is whether some poor countries lose from trade liberalization, a possibility illustrated by the end of global quotas on textiles and apparel at the start of [2005]. In the 1980s and early 1990s, developing countries pressed for these quotas to be lifted, hoping to boost exports to rich countries. But in the 15 years between their demanding this reform and getting it, the emergence of China as a trading superpower has altered the picture. Many poor countries would have been better off keeping their quotas, meager as they were, rather than venturing into a quota-free world in which China corners the market.

This phenomenon isn't true only for textiles. Lots of poor countries enjoy protected access to rich markets, extended via special bilateral and regional trade deals; global trade liberalization would erode the value of those preferences. If the United States abolished its sugar quotas, for example, efficient producers such as Brazil, Thailand and Colombia would gain market share. But inefficient producers, some of which actually import sugar in order to reexport it to the United States because of the quota-induced price gap, would be cut out of the market.

What's true for quotas is also true for subsidies. Ending rich countries' agricultural subsidies would reduce farm output in the United States and Europe, and less output would boost global prices. That would be great for developing countries that export food, such as Brazil and Argentina. But as Arvind Panagariya of Columbia University points out, nearly all of the world's poorest countries are net importers of food. Higher global prices might actually hurt them.

The second troubling question concerns the impact of free trade within poor countries. Even if a country as a whole benefits, the poorest groups or regions in that country may not. For example, suppose that rich countries abolish farm subsidies and quotas, so that global food prices rise. This will benefit farmers in developing countries who produce more food than they need to feed themselves—their surplus produce will bring in more revenue. But it will harm farmers who grow too little to feed themselves and who do non-farm work to earn wages and top up their diet. Most African farmers fall into this second category.

The Need for Complementary Policies

Rich-country politicians, who already bend over backward to please domestic protectionist interests, will no doubt seize on these questions to justify further obduracy. But this is exactly the wrong reaction. For one thing, the gains from trade outweigh the losses; for another, today's losers may become tomorrow's winners, given time to adapt to liberalization. Moreover, the conundrums that I've described don't show why trade is bad. They show why it has to be backed up with complementary policies.

Some of these policies are comfortable extensions of the free-trade philosophy. A formidable team of economists directed by [University of California at] Berkeley's Ann Harrison is about to come out with a volume titled "Globalization and Poverty"; a central message is that free trade works best for countries with labor mobility. For example, India's dramatic trade liberalization in the 1990s produced equally dramatic strides against poverty. But because Indian workers move surprisingly little between industries and regions, people in sectors that contracted as a result of the lifting of tariffs were trapped. Liberals who seek to "soften" trade deals by writing mobility-restricting labor regulations into them need to rethink their strategy.

Trade, though good, is not a panacea.

But the other policy necessary to complement free trade may force new thinking on some parts of the right, because it comes down to more development assistance. Rather than maintain farm subsidies that punish Argentine and Brazilian exporters, for example, rich countries should get rid of the subsidies—and then cushion the blow to food-importing countries by increasing aid to them. If just half of the $350 billion currently spent on farm subsidies were converted into development aid, official foreign assistance would triple. By spending a chunk of that money on agricultural research targeted at Africa, a woefully neglected field, rich countries could score a triple win—for African farmers, for Brazilians and Argentines, and for their own taxpayers.

Equally, aid offers the best way out of the trade-preferences dilemma. It's tempting to rig the rules so that China doesn't corner the market in textiles: Central America is nearer to home, Africa is especially poor, the Middle East has terrorism. But rewarding friends with trade preferences can be self-defeating in the end. Pretty soon so many regions get "special" access that nobody is really special. Moreover, preference deals generate onerous red tape: African-made clothing gets duty-free access to the United States, but to qualify it has to show that its constituent parts were not made in China and then assembled in Africa, and arguments as to what constitutes a constituent part can employ battalions of lawyers. It's far better, in other words, to grant everybody access free of red tape, and then to give some regions a helping hand with carefully designed aid programs.

[In 2000], large chunks of political opinion believed that trade was bad for poor countries; thankfully, that delusion has receded. But today, we must guard against the opposite mistake. Trade, though good, is not a panacea.

CHAPTER 3

Can Democracy Succeed in Developing Nations?

Chapter Preface

U.S. president George W. Bush has promoted democracy in the Middle East as a way to foster peace, stability, and prosperity in that troubled and underdeveloped region. Historically, democratic countries have seldom gone to war with each other and have been successful economically, so the Bush administration has seen democratization as the antidote for centuries of Mideast political volatility and poverty. In addition, President Bush no doubt hoped that new democratic nations in the oil-rich Middle East would tend to be allies of the United States, the world's most powerful democracy, helping to ensure American access to vast oil and gas reserves critical for future U.S. energy needs.

The democratization strategy, however, has taken a direction that U.S. officials did not anticipate—one that many political observers say may be empowering radical Islamic elements that are hostile to the United States and its interests. In December 2005, for example, Egyptian voters strongly supported the Muslim Brotherhood, a radical Islamic party, and in Lebanon, the electorate has given increasing support to Hezbollah, an Islamic terrorist group supported by Iran. In Iraq's elections following the U.S. removal of dictator Saddam Hussein, Iraqis installed a pro-Iranian Islamist from the Shia religious sect as prime minister.

Meanwhile, in a January 2006 election conducted in the Palestinian territories, Palestinian voters rejected the more moderate, U.S.–supported Fatah party led by Palestinian president Mahmoud Abbas, instead giving a majority of their votes to the Islamist group Hamas. Hamas won 76 of the 132 seats in the Palestinian Legislative Council, with Fatah receiving only 43 seats. Hamas is listed as a terrorist group by the United States and many other countries, has admitted responsibility for numerous suicide bomb attacks on Israeli soldiers and citizens, and has historically refused even to recognize Israel's right to exist as a nation. Hamas, however, has largely abided by a cease-fire brokered in March 2005.

The Hamas election victory gave the group the right to choose the next Palestinian cabinet and thus set up a power struggle between the council and President Abbas, who had been elected to a four-year term. Abbas's Fatah supporters occupy many government posts and make up most of the Palestinian security forces that are charged with keeping order in the Palestinian territories. Immediately after the election, Abbas tried to negotiate with Hamas to set up a unity government, but that effort quickly failed. Since then, the two sides have engaged in a political tug-of-war that has, increasingly, erupted into actual fighting and street violence. In December 2006, Abbas called for new elections and a few weeks later declared Hamas's six thousand-member military force illegal—steps designed to eventually oust Hamas from the government. Hamas responded by vowing to double the militia's size. Many political commentators worried that a full-fledged Palestinian civil war could result.

The election of Hamas shocked officials in the Bush administration and effectively stopped all efforts by the United States to push its allies in the Middle East—countries such as Saudi Arabia, Jordan, and Egypt—to implement democratic reforms. Hamas's new position of power also created tough new obstacles for American hopes to reinvigorate the stalled Middle East peace process, a decades-long effort to negotiate an end to the conflict between Israel and the Palestinians over land that Israel occupied in the 1967 Arab-Israeli War. As a result of Hamas's rise to power, Western countries such as the United States and the European Union cut their assistance to the Palestinian Authority, the government of the Palestinians, depriving them of almost a billion dollars of desperately needed funds. The United States also has sent arms to Fatah and reportedly has been urging President Abbas to confront Hamas.

Some analysts had hoped that Hamas's entry into mainstream politics, perhaps combined with the cutoff in financial support, would cause the group to become moderate in its politics. So far, however, Hamas has not softened its position on Israel, renounced violence, nor given up its arms. Shortly after its election victory, Hamas leader Khalid Mechal said the group would be willing to negotiate with Israel, but only if Israel agreed to a series of conditions, one of which was withdrawing to its 1967 borders, which would mean leaving the Israeli-occupied Arab territories of Gaza, the West Bank, and the Golan Heights. The Hamas offer was summarily rejected by Israel. In late November 2006, Hamas announced that it would agree to a six-month window of peace negotiations with Israel, but warned that if negotiations did not produce an agreement for a Palestinian state within that time period, the group might launch a new round of fighting—a threat that no doubt would include the resumption of suicide bomb attacks against Israel. A year after the elections, tensions are only growing among Palestinians, with no peace negotiations under way with Israel.

This situation presents a dilemma for the United States and its allies. On the one hand, U.S. officials do not want to work with a group that it considers terroristic unless Hamas agrees to recognize Israel and renounce violence. Yet Hamas has been democratically elected and appears to have the strong support of the Palestinian people, putting the United States in the position of opposing an elected government—a position at odds with its announced pro-democracy policy. Despite this U.S. opposition, the future remains uncertain because Hamas does not appear ready to give up its new power easily.

What seems clear from the Hamas example is that democracy does not promote peace and stability in all cases. The pros and cons of democratization for developing regions of the world are further illuminated by the authors in this chapter.

Democracy Is the Path to a Safer and Better World

George W. Bush

George W. Bush is the forty-third president of the United States.

We gather at a time of tremendous opportunity for the U.N [United Nations] and for all peaceful nations. For decades, the circle of liberty and security and development has been expanding in our world. This progress has brought unity to Europe, self-government to Latin America and Asia, and new hope to Africa. Now we have the historic chance to widen the circle even further, to fight radicalism and terror with justice and dignity, to achieve a true peace, founded on human freedom.

The United Nations and my country share the deepest commitments. Both the American Declaration of Independence and the Universal Declaration of Human Rights proclaim the equal value and dignity of every human life. That dignity is honored by the rule of law, limits on the power of the state, respect for women, protection of private property, free speech, equal justice, and religious tolerance. That dignity is dishonored by oppression, corruption, tyranny, bigotry, terrorism and all violence against the innocent. And both of our founding documents affirm that this bright line between justice and injustice—between right and wrong—is the same in every age, and every culture, and every nation.

Wise governments also stand for these principles for very practical and realistic reasons. We know that dictators are quick to choose aggression, while free nations strive to resolve differences in peace. We know that oppressive governments support terror, while free governments fight the terrorists in

George W. Bush, address to the 59th U.N. General Assembly, September 21, 2004.
http://usinfo.state.gov.

their midst. We know that free peoples embrace progress and life, instead of becoming the recruits for murderous ideologies.

Every nation that wants peace will share the benefits of a freer world. And every nation that seeks peace has an obligation to help build that world. Eventually, there is no safe isolation from terror networks, or failed states that shelter them, or outlaw regimes, or weapons of mass destruction. Eventually, there is no safety in looking away, seeking the quiet life by ignoring the struggles and oppression of others.

In this young century, our world needs a new definition of security. Our security is not merely found in spheres of influence, or some balance of power. The security of our world is found in the advancing rights of mankind. . . .

Freedom is finding a way in Iraq and Afghanistan—and we must continue to show our commitment to democracies in those nations.

The Promise of Democracy

Because we believe in human dignity, peaceful nations must stand for the advance of democracy. No other system of government has done more to protect minorities, to secure the rights of labor, to raise the status of women, or to channel human energy to the pursuits of peace. We've witnessed the rise of democratic governments in predominantly Hindu and Muslim, Buddhist, Jewish and Christian cultures. Democratic institutions have taken root in modern societies, and in traditional societies. When it comes to the desire for liberty and justice, there is no clash of civilizations. People everywhere are capable of freedom, and worthy of freedom.

Finding the full promise of representative government takes time, as America has found in two centuries of debate and struggle. Nor is there . . . only one form of representative government—because democracies, by definition, take on the unique character of the peoples that create them. Yet this much we know with certainty: The desire for freedom resides in every human heart. And that desire cannot be contained forever by prison walls, or martial laws, or secret police. Over time, and across the Earth, freedom will find a way.

Terrorists . . . know that a free Iraq in the heart of the Middle East will be a decisive blow against their ambitions for that region.

Iraq and Afghanistan

Freedom is finding a way in Iraq and Afghanistan—and we must continue to show our commitment to democracies in those nations. The liberty that many have won at a cost must be secured. As members of the United Nations, we all have a stake in the success of the world's newest democracies.

Not long ago, outlaw regimes in Baghdad [Iraq] and Kabul [Afghanistan] threatened the peace and sponsored terrorists. These regimes destabilized one of the world's most vital—and most volatile—regions. They brutalized their peoples, in defiance of all civilized norms. Today, the Iraqi and Afghan people are on the path to democracy and freedom. The governments that are rising will pose no threat to others. Instead of harboring terrorists, they're fighting terrorist groups. And this progress is good for the long-term security of us all.

The Afghan people are showing extraordinary courage under difficult conditions. They're fighting to defend their nation from Taliban [the ousted fundamentalist Muslim regime] holdouts, and helping to strike against the terrorist killers. They're reviving their economy. They've adopted a constitution that protects the rights of all, while honoring their nation's most cherished traditions. More than 10 million Afghan citizens—over 4 million of them women—are now registered to vote in [the] next . . . presidential election. To any who still would question whether Muslim societies can be democratic societies, the Afghan people are giving their answer.

Since the last meeting of this General Assembly, the people of Iraq have regained sovereignty. Today, in this hall, the Prime Minister of Iraq and his delegation represent a country that has rejoined the community of nations. The [Iraqi] government . . . has earned the support of every nation that believes in self-determination and desires peace. And under Security Council resolutions 1511 and 1546, the world is providing that support. The U.N., and its member nations, must respond to [Iraq's] request, and do more to help build an Iraq that is secure, democratic, federal, and free.

A democratic Iraq has ruthless enemies, because terrorists know the stakes in that country. They know that a free Iraq in the heart of the Middle East will be a decisive blow against their ambitions for that region. So a terrorist group associated with al-Qaeda is now one of the main groups killing the innocent in Iraq today—conducting a campaign of bombings against civilians, and the beheadings of bound men. Coalition forces now serving in Iraq are confronting the terrorists and foreign fighters, so peaceful nations around the world will never have to face them within our own borders.

Our coalition is standing beside a growing Iraqi security force. The NATO [North Atlantic Treaty Organization] Alliance is providing vital training to that force. More than 35 nations have contributed money and expertise to help rebuild Iraq's infrastructure. And as the Iraqi interim government moves toward national elections, officials from the United Nations are helping Iraqis build the infrastructure of democracy. These selfless people are doing heroic work, and are carrying on the great legacy of Sergio de Mello [assassinated UN High Commissioner for Human Rights].

As we have seen in other countries, one of the main terrorist goals is to undermine, disrupt, and influence election outcomes. We can expect terrorist attacks to escalate as Afghanistan and Iraq approach national elections. The work ahead is demanding. But these difficulties will not shake our conviction that the future of Afghanistan and Iraq is a future of liberty. The proper response to difficulty is not to retreat, it is to prevail.

[Iraq and Afghanistan] will be a model for the broader Middle East, a region where millions have been denied basic human rights and simple justice.

The advance of freedom always carries a cost, paid by the bravest among us. America mourns the losses to our nation, and to many others. And today, I assure every friend of Afghanistan and Iraq, and every enemy of liberty: We will stand with the people of Afghanistan and Iraq until their hopes of freedom and security are fulfilled.

Democracy Throughout the Middle East and Elsewhere

These two nations will be a model for the broader Middle East, a region where millions have been denied basic human rights and simple justice. For too long, many nations, including my own, tolerated, even excused, oppression in the Middle East in the name of stability. Oppression became common, but stability never arrived. We must take a different approach. We must help the reformers of the Middle East as they work for freedom, and strive to build a community of peaceful, democratic nations.

This commitment to democratic reform is essential to resolving the Arab-Israeli conflict. Peace will not be achieved by Palestinian rulers who intimidate opposition, tolerate corruption, and maintain ties to terrorist groups. The long-suffering

Palestinian people deserve better. They deserve true leaders capable of creating and governing a free and peaceful Palestinian state.

Even after the setbacks and frustrations of recent months, goodwill and hard effort can achieve the promise of the road map to peace. Those who would lead a new Palestinian state should adopt peaceful means to achieve the rights of their people, and create the reformed institutions of a stable democracy. Arab states should end incitement in their own media, cut off public and private funding for terrorism, and establish normal relations with Israel. Israel should impose a settlement freeze, dismantle unauthorized outposts, end the daily humiliation of the Palestinian people, and avoid any actions that prejudice final negotiations. And world leaders should withdraw all favor and support from any Palestinian ruler who fails his people and betrays their cause.

The democratic hopes we see growing in the Middle East are growing everywhere. In the words of the Burmese democracy advocate, Aung San Suu Kyi: "We do not accept the notion that democracy is a Western value. To the contrary; democracy simply means good government rooted in responsibility, transparency, and accountability." Here at the United Nations, you know this to be true. In recent years, this organization has helped create a new democracy in East Timor, and the U.N. has aided other nations in making the transition to self-rule.

Democracy Fund

Because I believe the advance of liberty is the path to both a safer and better world, today I propose establishing a Democracy Fund within the United Nations. This is a great calling for this great organization. The fund would help countries lay the foundations of democracy by instituting the rule of law and independent courts, a free press, political parties and trade unions. Money from the fund would also help set up voter precincts and polling places, and support the work of election monitors. To show our commitment to the new Democracy Fund, the United States will make an initial contribution. I urge other nations to contribute, as well.

Today, I've outlined a broad agenda to advance human dignity, and enhance the security of all of us. The defeat of terror, the protection of human rights, the spread of prosperity, the advance of democracy—these causes, these ideals, call us to great work in the world. Each of us alone can only do so much. Together, we can accomplish so much more.

History will honor the high ideals of this organization. The charter states them with clarity: "to save succeeding generations from the scourge of war," "to reaffirm faith in fundamental human rights," "to promote social progress and better standards of life in larger freedom." Let history also record that our generation of leaders followed through on these ideals, even in adversity. Let history show that in a decisive decade, members of the United Nations did not grow weary in our duties, or waver in meeting them. I'm confident that this young century will be liberty's century. I believe we will rise to this moment, because I know the character of so many nations and leaders represented here today. And I have faith in the transforming power of freedom.

Islam Is Compatible
with Democracy

Helle Dale

*Helle Dale is a foreign affairs analyst at The Heritage Founda-
tion, a conservative think tank. A former editor and columnist
for the* Washington Times *newspaper, Dale also is a media fellow at the Hoover Institution at Stanford University, serves on
the board of the Institute on Political Journalism at Georgetown
University, and is a member of the Council on Foreign Relations.*

Editor's Note*: Following the January 2005 Iraqi elections, the
Iraqi government named Ibrahim al-Jaafari as prime minister
and adopted a constitution, which was approved by voters in
October 2005. In December 2005, Iraq held a second set of elections to elect a permanent legislature, and in April 2006, a new
prime minister, Nouri al-Maliki, was selected. Al-Qaeda leader
Abu Musab Zarqawi was killed by U.S. warplanes in June 2006.*

Is Islam culturally and religiously incompatible with democracy? Elections in Afghanistan and Iraq surely ought to
put an end to that debate—at least as far as the desire of ordinary Muslims are concerned to vote and be heard. You would
have to have a heart of stone not to be moved and inspired by
the sight of Iraqis flocking to the polls on [January 30, 2005,]
defying suicide bombers and threats to their lives as well as
those of their children. Even the hardened skeptics in the
American media found themselves carried away by the courage of the Iraqi people.

Big losers in [the January 30, 2005] . . . election for an interim Iraqi government were the terrorists, particularly murderous thugs like Osama bin Laden and his "mini-me," Abu
Musab Zarqawi [former head of the terrorist group al Qaeda

in Iraq]. Beyond that, the losers are the critics and the nay-sayers in our part of the world who did not believe elections could take place, or thought they should have been postponed into the indefinite future. And those who advocate immediate American disengagement. The big winners were the Iraqi people and the [George W.] Bush administration, which has staked huge political capital on a successful election.

Losing Fear

Once people lose their fear, anything can happen. Eyewitnesses in Iraq have compared the mood in many cities to the mood in Eastern Europe when communism collapsed. In the end, over 60 percent of Iraqis voted, which is about equal to the last American election. In the recent Palestinian election, which was hailed as a triumph the world over, 55 percent of eligible voters went to the polls.

Fear of violence dominated the first hours of polling in Iraq, but then people started pouring out. When a young suicide bomber blew himself and seven other people to pieces outside a polling station at a girls' school in Baghdad, voters were not deterred. Walking around the remains of the bombing, they just kept coming.

The question whether Islam and democracy [are] compatible already has an affirmative answer in countries like Turkey and Indonesia.

One reluctant voter in Baghdad, auto mechanic Wamidh al-Zubaidy, told *The Washington Times*, that he decided to vote in spite of threats from masked men to burn down his house. "Then I remembered my brother who Saddam [Hussein] executed," he said. "I felt a power inside myself, and there was a voice telling me, 'this should not happen to my son or to any Iraqi.' . . . . I voted with my wife, and we put it in God's hands."

Now, this is not even the beginning of the end for the United States engagement in Iraq, but perhaps it is the end of the beginning, to borrow Winston Churchill's phrase. Voting in the Sunni triangle in the center of the country was sparse. To the Sunnis, the dominant tribe under Saddam Hussein, Sunday must have been more like a day of mourning, as Shiite and Kurdish communities celebrated freedom from oppression.

The Challenge Ahead

The great question is now whether Iraq's emerging politicians can become democrats and work together probably in a coalition to create Iraq's first post-Ba'athist [Party] constitution. Secular Interim Prime Minister Ayad Allawi [who was succeeded by Ibrahim al-Jaafari and later Nouri al-Maliki] and the United Iraqi Alliance, which represents Shiite parties, will have to work together. They will also have to find ways of including the Sunnis. This is going to be difficult and complicated business.

And beyond that, there is always the threat of the fanatics and the remnants of Saddam's forces that will be waging war from the sidelines. They remain deadly, though recent reports have downplayed their level of organization.

The question whether Islam and democracy [are] compatible already has an affirmative answer in countries like Turkey and Indonesia. Whether it is compatible with Islam as practiced in the Arab world has been a matter of intense debate . . . since September 11, [2001]. Since then, we have been exposed to the ugly, fanatic face of radical Islam, through the indiscriminate killing of Westerners, assorted "infidels" and fellow Muslims.

Before [the January 30, 2005] election bizarre antidemocratic proclamations were issued by terrorist cleric Abu Musab Zarqawi, whose sole claim to fame has been to mastermind appalling acts of terrorism and cruelty against Iraqi civilians and children, allied forces in Iraq and westerners kidnapped by his followers. His threats were somewhat reminiscent of Osama bin Laden's attempts at influencing the American election through long-distance threats. Zarqawi railed against candidates and voters alike, denouncing democracy as an "evil principle" because it is based on "freedom of religion," "freedom of speech," and "separation of religion and politics."

Clearly Zarqawi and Muslim clerics of a like mind understand that democracy loosens the grip of religious leaders on their followers and empowers individuals to practice their politics and their religion as they see fit. No wonder they are afraid of its power.

President Bush's Mideast Democracy Policy Could Succeed

Duncan Currie

Duncan Currie is a reporter at the Weekly Standard, *a conservative political magazine.*

Remember the "Arab Spring"? That ephemeral blip of, oh, six or seven weeks ... [in] February and March [2005] when scattered [George W.] Bush critics second-guessed their opposition to the Iraq war and the president's Mideast-democracy project? Given that most Americans now deem the war a mistake, it's easy to forget that ... conservatives and liberals alike were hailing George W. Bush as the 400-pound gorilla of a nascent transformation in Arab politics.

A Period of Success for Democratization

Those were heady days for the administration. During the infant stages of Beirut's "Cedar Revolution," Lebanese Druze chieftain Walid Jumblatt—hardly a pro-American stooge—remarked that the January 30th Iraqi elections had torn down a "Berlin Wall" [that had separated Communist East Berlin from democratic West Berlin] of autarkic sclerosis and midwifed "a new Arab world." Spurred by the killing of their popular prime minister, thousands of Lebanese took to the streets in an astounding spectacle. The stock character in Jumblatt's "new Arab world" was a youthful demonstrator baying for responsive governance. Lebanon's [Syrian president] Assad-backed puppet soon resigned, and Syria's occupying troops began packing their bags. Meanwhile, Hosni Mubarak, Egypt's president-for-life, sanctioned multi-party elections, Iraqi crowds gathered to denounce terrorism, and notable swathes of Palestinians rebuked the [Yasir] Arafat-linked kleptocrats running their affairs.

Amidst the progress in Iraq, the spate of 1989-style "people power" protests, and Mubarak's unprecedented call for a free vote, many American liberals—along with a host of their counterparts in Canada and Western Europe—found themselves wondering if the toppling of Saddam Hussein and the subsequent push for Iraqi democracy might have been worth the trouble after all. One by one, like falling dominoes, a veritable "Who's Who" of Bush bashers stepped forward to request a sizable helping of crow.

Toronto Star columnist Richard Gwyn went first. "It is time to set down in type the most difficult sentence in the English language," Gwyn wrote after watching Iraqis trek to the polls. "That sentence is short and simple. It is this: Bush was right." Well then. *The New York Times* editorial page gave Bush his due—the administration could "claim a healthy share of the credit" for having "boldly proclaimed the cause of Middle East democracy at a time when few in the West thought it had any realistic chance." Not to be outdone was Comedy Central's philosopher-comic, Jon Stewart. "What if Bush . . . has been right about this all along?" he asked on his *Daily Show*. "I feel like my worldview will not sustain itself and I may . . . implode." One day, Stewart joked, "my kid's gonna go to a high school named after [Bush]."

America's campaign for democracy in the Middle East is making progress.

Across the pond, Claus Christian Malzahn wrote a remarkable cover story for Germany's *Der Spiegel*. "Germany loves to criticize U.S. President George W. Bush's Middle East policies—just like Germany loved to criticize former president Ronald Reagan," Malzahn wrote. "But Reagan, when he demanded that Mikhail Gorbachev remove the Berlin Wall, turned out to be right. Could history repeat itself?" Nor were French and British leftists immune to the contagion. "The merit of George Bush is to have held firm to his discourse from the day after 9/11," acknowledged an editorial in *Le Monde*. "He developed the idea that the Muslim peoples have the right to freedom, to democracy, to prosperity." London's *Independent* captured the baffled sentiments of many Europeans with its front-page headline, "Was Bush Right After All?" . . .

Recent Progress for Democracy in the Middle East

What exactly has changed since then? The Iraqi political process continues apace. For those keen on "timetables," America has yet to miss a single deadline in managing Iraq's post-Saddam transition. The Sunni Arabs, who now realize how foolish their election boycott proved [in the first election], turned out in droves to vote in the October 15th [2005] constitutional referendum (albeit, in most cases, to cast a "no" ballot) and are expected to vote in even greater numbers in . . . parliamentary poll[s]. After a recent visit to Iraq, [Connecticut] Sen. Joe Lieberman wrote in the *Wall Street Journal* that he "was thrilled to see a vigorous political campaign, and a large number of independent television stations and newspapers covering it."

Elsewhere in the Mideast, Egypt held its first multi-candidate presidential election [in] September [2005] which, though tainted by the ruling party's shenanigans, nevertheless marked a watershed. "The country's old authoritarian system has broken apart," reported *Washington Post* columnist David Ignatius from Cairo. Absent the Bush administration's "nagging," opined the *Economist*, "Mr. Mubarak would never have considered for a second that he should let himself be challenged at the polls for the top job. However clumsy in its promotion and debatable its motives, America's campaign for democracy in the Middle East is making progress."

Indeed, we've also had parliamentary elections in Lebanon, baby steps toward reform in Saudi Arabia, amplified pressure on Syria, and liberal sproutings in Morocco, Palestine, Jordan, Kuwait, Bahrain, and Qatar. On the hearts-and-minds front, a July 2005 survey by the Pew Global Attitudes Project found that "large and growing majorities" of Moroccans (83 percent), Jordanians (80 percent), and Lebanese (83 percent) "say democracy can work well and is not just for the West." Meanwhile, more than 200,000 irate Jordanians responded to [the November 2005] Amman hotel bombings by pouring into the streets to protest. Chants of "Burn in hell, Abu Musab al-Zarqawi!" and "Death to al Qaeda!" could reportedly be heard.

Many Americans expected ballots, purple fingers, and Muslim people power to summarily quell the Iraqi insurgency. If so, they were disappointed.

Admittedly, the progress has at times been uneven. For example, Egypt's recent parliamentary elections were marred by bloody clashes between voters and riot police, which resulted in several deaths. This smacked of the old order, with Mubarak's goons blocking or attacking polling places in many opposition strongholds. Still, those elections yielded historic results for Egyptian pluralism.

"To venture into the Arab world" observes Johns Hopkins professor Fouad Ajami, "is to travel into Bush Country." Ajami—who [in 2005] spent several weeks in Qatar, Kuwait, Jordan, and Iraq—reports encountering "people from practically all Arab lands" engaged in "a great debate about the possibility of freedom and liberty." He also "met Syrians in the know who admitted that the fear of American power, and the example of American forces flushing Saddam Hussein out of his spider hole, now drive Syrian policy. They hang on George Bush's words in Damascus, I was told: the rulers wondering if Iraq was a crystal ball in which they could glimpse their future."

The Final Verdict

So what explains all the pessimism stateside? It could be that many Americans expected ballots, purple fingers, and Muslim people power to summarily quell the Iraqi insurgency. If so, they were disappointed. Car explosions, suicide bombers, mortar blasts, and kidnappings remain a pervasive reality in the Sunni Triangle. And more than 2,000 U.S. servicemen have now made the ultimate sacrifice. That this number is comparatively low by the standards of prior American wars offers no comfort to families who've lost a relative or friend.

But what if U.S. intervention did create "a new Arab world," as Walid Jumblatt claimed? What if it did vanquish the Middle Eastern "Berlin Wall"? And what if it saved untold Americans—and Arabs—from far deadlier wars in the future? While we mourn each and every U.S. casualty, we must never lose sight of what the American military has accomplished. Despite all the setbacks, Iraq's budding democracy continues to move ahead. So does the training of Iraq's fledgling security forces, a prerequisite for any significant withdrawal of U.S. troops.

We won't know the final verdict on . . . [Bush's] radical foreign policy until farther down the road—not for years, perhaps not even for decades.

As for the Bush Doctrine's loftier goal—to reform Arab politics and drain the swamp from which Islamic terrorism draws its chief ideological firepower—that no longer seems a fool's errand. Even the most determined naysayer must acknowledge what American policy—coupled with felicitous circumstances—has wrought. George W. Bush deposed Saddam to remove a dangerous tyranny and promote U.S. interests in a vital region. He may wind up creating the first Arab democracy and changing the political culture of the Middle East— which would deal a severe blow to the forces of militant Islam.

But Bush's is a rearview-mirror presidency: We won't know the final verdict on his radical foreign policy until farther down the road—not for years, perhaps not even for decades. Of course, the preliminary vindication or repudiation of the Bush Doctrine hinges on Iraq. As Joshua Muravchik has argued in *Commentary*, losing Iraq to the jihadists and Saddamists today would be far more disastrous than losing South Vietnam to the Communists was in 1975. "Vietnam was always a distant corner of the cold war, whose epicenter lay in Berlin," Muravchik writes. "But Iraq is right in the heart of the Arab world, and it is now the central front of World War IV. Defeat there would be more akin to a cold-war defeat in Germany than in Indochina."

Democratic Policies Are Contributing to Political and Economic Instability in Many Developing Countries

John Mulaa

John Mulaa is a columnist with Kenya's second-largest newspaper, the Sunday Standard.

Is the spread of democracy hitting inevitable bumps and does democracy have serious unintended consequences in some places where it has been hastily planted? These and a number of other questions have been the central preoccupation of a Yale University political scientist, Amy Chua.

Chua has established a reputation as something of a contrarian. At a time when most academics and think tanks were churning out opuses and treatises claiming how wonderful democracy would be for all societies at all times, Chua, an American of Philippine-Chinese descent, published her contrary book *World on Fire: How Exporting Free Market Democracy Breeds Ethnic Hatred and Global Instability*. In the book, Chua claimed that the world was refusing to scrutinise the consequences of exporting liberal democracy to ill-prepared societies, all in the hope that it will turn out right in the end. They might indeed, according to Chua, but in the meantime, mayhem has been sown all over the globe. I have listened and watched Chua at length on C-Span, a public affairs television channel, and she has repeatedly made what she means clear. Her thesis is by no means a defence of the dwindling band of autocrats across the globe. She is a liberal democrat to the core, but a cautionary one who believes more thought and care needs to go into some ideas before they are foisted on unsuspecting places that end up paying a very heavy price.

Democracy and Instability

Chua's . . . conclusions are startling if rather obvious in hindsight: the spread of laissez-faire capitalism and democracy can hasten political and economic instability at least in the short run. She notes that across developing countries that have recently embraced democracy either willingly or through a combination of outside and internal pressures, the democratic road once embarked upon ushers a host of countervailing factors that threaten the very existence of the countries.

In combination with the liberal market orthodoxy of urging the stripping of functions from states, the result has been severely circumscribed and weak states that can barely stand. Gurus of free-markets and unbounded liberalism such as [economist] Milton Friedman and [political scientist] Francis Fukuyama are reportedly having second thoughts after witnessing the social wreckage that have been partly blamed on uncritical application of the much fangled ideas.

There is a nascent backlash against and disillusionment with democracy across a swathe of Latin America.

In Venezuela, for instance, democratic elections propelled Hugo Chavez to the presidency but in the process widened the country's social and economic fissures. The traditional ruling elite, Venezuelans of European ancestry who have long dominated the society, initiated intense and well orchestrated opposition to their nemesis. As a result, democracy has almost been stopped in its tracks in Venezuela. The country is preparing for a referendum on possible recall of Hugo Chavez who still enjoys wide support among the pardo—Venezuelans of non-European ancestry. There is talk of violence in the air.

Reports also suggest that aside from Venezuela, there is a nascent backlash against and disillusionment with democracy across a swathe of Latin America. In Bolivia, an ardently pro-market president was driven out of office by a proletariat enraged by his tendency to privatise everything in sight. Peasants and urban workers in several Latin American countries are reportedly talking nostalgically of strong man rule that they claim at least maintained a modicum of order.

According to Chua, what is transpiring in Venezuela and Bolivia are no exceptions. It is a global phenomenon—almost never acknowledged—of the democratic process being used by majorities to dislodge affluent ethnic minorities who, for a variety of reasons, tend to do well under market conditions and to dominate economically the indigenous majorities. (Chinese in Indonesia and Malaysia, whites in Zimbabwe and Indians in Kenya, for example). A cocktail of democracy and simmering ethnic hatred has produced only one known outcome so far: stunted countries unable to move ahead or if they have done so, it has been by jettisoning the tenets of liberal democracy. Malaysia simply enacted into law a stringent quota system in almost every sphere of life to dilute the power of its citizens of Chinese descent.

The Democratic Experience in Africa

The democratic experience of several African countries in the past decade or so would seem to confirm Chua's central point, that it is not enough to unload democracy on societies and expect them to make a successful go at it. Success has been the exception rather than the rule. What is clearly emerging is that the success stories cannot be replicated elsewhere because of their unique causes.

The majority is flailing about, neither stable nor democratic, minus the order that sometimes accrues from strong man rule. Zambia was among the first African countries to take the plunge at the outset of the democratic "wind of change" in Africa. Kenya and Malawi were stragglers whose ruling elites were dragged screaming to the guillotine of democracy. Both countries are struggling to keep their footing along the democratic path and, so far, the evidence is mixed as to which way they will go.

Democracy . . . has to be built bottom up by first spreading as widely as possible the benefits of the hoped for system of government.

Uganda, the holdout that is still enmeshed in a no-party democracy, will inevitably be pushed onto the precarious path of liberal democracy. Given the country's history, there is no telling how it will all turn out, but it is not unreasonable to suggest that it could all go wrong and force the country back to a state of nature where it was not too long ago.

Democracy from the Bottom Up

Is Chua suggesting that democracy stands little chance in developing countries? Her answer is a qualified No. Democracy, she maintains, has to be built bottom up by first spreading as widely as possible the benefits of the hoped for system of government.

In other words, the revolution must come from below, with genuine international assistance. As long as rapacious elites are kept in check, their power can be destroyed over time by strengthening the economic means of the populations. Revolutions of the kind the world has witnessed lately may be easier to make but are not likely to produce lasting positive results.

Elections Alone Will Not Create Democratic States

Daveed Gartenstein-Ross and Nir Boms

Daveed Gartenstein-Ross is a counterterrorism consultant and attorney. Nir Boms is vice president of the Center for Freedom in the Middle East, a coalition of political and advocacy groups, individuals, and scholars from the Middle East working to uphold freedom.

When Americans learned that 41-year-old Afgan citizen Abdul Rahman could be put to death for converting to Christianity, they were outraged. [Former convicted Watergate attorney and founder of a Christian prison ministry] Chuck Colson spoke for many when he wrote, "Is this the fruit of democracy? Is this why we have shed American blood and invested American treasure to set a people free?" (Although Abdul Rahman was ultimately whisked away to the safety of Italy, the apostasy laws [laws against abandoning the Islamic faith] used to charge him haven't been repealed.) When the Abdul Rahman case is added to Hamas's [an Islamic terrorist group] electoral victory in the Palestinian territories and the Muslim Brotherhood's [a radical Islamist religious movement] gains in Egypt's recent parliamentary elections, a disturbing trend emerges: the rise of illiberal democracy in the Middle East.

Democratic Elections Are Not Enough

Elections are an integral part of a democracy—but they are not a substitute for a liberal democratic culture. Almost half of today's "democratizing" countries can be classified as what

[*Newsweek* editor] Fareed Zakaria dubs "illiberal democracies": Although they hold regular elections, they also violate their citizens' human rights, political liberties, and religious freedom. The George W. Bush administration, which has taken on the cause of advancing democracy in the Middle East, should be particularly concerned by these developments.

The theory behind pushing Middle Eastern democracy is that of the safety valve: If Middle Easterners have a say in their governance, the theory goes, they will be less likely to turn to violence. But recent events have called this theory into question. Will democratization end up unwittingly empowering the enemies of the West?

Empowered Islamists will serve as obstacles on the road to greater U.S. security.

If the United States continues down its current path, it may well end up doing just that. Right now there is only one institution in the Middle East in which citizens can safely gather and criticize the government: the mosque. Fundamentalist parties have been the strongest critics of the corrupt governments that fill the region, and voters often find that if they want to protest the ruling regimes, they are forced to vote for the Islamist opposition.

Promoting U.S. Security

Empowered Islamists will serve as obstacles on the road to greater U.S. security. It is only after the rise of liberal institutions such as freedom of speech, freedom of the press, freedom of assembly, and freedom of religion that Middle Eastern elections can provide the vibrant alternatives that we expect truly democratic systems to provide. But how can we effectively promote liberal institutions?

Two important realizations are needed. The first is that a democratic culture cannot be built overnight—especially not in a region which has such a long history of oppressive and authoritarian government. The second is that democracy must be measured by the level of liberalism it engenders, not the number of ballots cast. As recent history shows, elections can be the continuation of autocracy by other means.

True, elections are easy to measure and can be quite dramatic: See the wave of purple-fingered citizens that marked Iraq's first democratic vote. But elections are not the most important indicator of a state's progression—and we may want to temper our enthusiasm for pushing them until the Middle East develops a more liberal culture.

To help promote liberalism, our policymakers need to improve their cultural literacy so they can more easily identify and effectively work with regional and local players devoted to the values of tolerance and political freedom. It took a revolution to create democracies in Europe and America—and it may take another revolution in the Middle East. But that revolution can only come from within, spearheaded by existing forces that already work toward democratization.

The United States needs to be careful in choosing which of these groups to support, as not all of them have the constituencies that they would like us to believe, and not all of them will be amenable to U.S. interest—or the interests of the citizens of their respective countries for that matter. By now, these groups have track records that can be examined on the merits. Policymakers should support those groups that seek, and are capable of contributing to, genuine democratic change.

The U.S. should also support expatriate movements. The democratization process seeks to bring about a new discourse that has been suppressed, both by the ruling elites and also by the Islamist opposition. Expatriate movements can help this new discourse take shape. The work of the Lebanese and Syrian expatriate communities, for example, has already proved effective in the context of the Syrian withdrawal from Lebanon.

Finally, official U.S. rhetoric should be adjusted to take account of the broader goal of promoting a liberal democratic culture. Official pronouncements shouldn't focus exclusively on elections. Rather, liberal institutions should be at the forefront of what representatives of the United States say on the world stage.

Ultimately, there is no magic bullet that can transform the Middle East's political culture with a single shot. But by taking concrete steps toward a viable long-term goal, we can give ourselves—and the citizens of the Middle East—the greatest chance of success.

The Prospects for Democracy in Iraq Are Dim

Charley Reese

Charley Reese is an American syndicated columnist who writes frequently about U.S. politics and foreign policy matters.

[President George W. Bush] believes that democracy can be implanted at the point of a gun and that, once implanted in Iraq, it will spread to the rest of the Middle East. He's wrong, in my opinion. If we analyze what makes us a free nation, we will see where he is wrong.

The Lack of Democratic Traditions

First and foremost, we have a 200-year tradition of the military bowing to civilian rule. Yes, I know it's in the Constitution, but the Constitution is just words on parchment. If the military men didn't believe it, they could easily take control of the country. They never have. They have never even tried or thought about it seriously. That is to their very great credit.

There is no such tradition in Iraq or in any of the Arab countries. A willingness to obey the civilian authorities even though you have the guns and they don't is not something that can be taught in a few weeks of training. Maybe this Iraqi army we are creating will stay in its barracks, and maybe it won't. Any old Middle East hand would bet that it won't.

Freedom of speech is another characteristic of our culture, which predates the American Revolution. Even we, however, sometimes infringe on free speech, especially in time of war. Again, there is no such tradition in Iraq or in the other Arab countries. Their tradition is that you are free to speak if the ruler says you can speak. Neither of Iraq's temporary governments—the one we appointed or the one the Iraqis elected—has been especially tolerant of Iraqi criticism.

Ironically, the greatest example of free speech and a free press in the Middle East is al-Jazeera television, which [former] Secretary of Defense Donald Rumsfeld and President Bush both seem to hate. They hate it because it reports what they don't want reported, which is, after all, the essence of a free press. To our everlasting shame, we bombed al-Jazeera's offices in Afghanistan and in Baghdad. The official lie that they were both accidents doesn't hold a teacup of water. The idea that two small offices in different countries but belonging to the same company could be hit from 15,000 feet by accident is improbable as hell.

It took several centuries for the ideas of freedom to take root in the United Kingdom and its offspring, which includes [the United States.]

Another irony, if you are into that sort of thing, is that the only democratically elected government in the Muslim part of that region is Iran's, and again, our government is definitely not happy about that.

A third characteristic of a free society is that the authorities must respect the rights of individuals. Even with our long tradition, that is a constant battle for us. Witness the charges of police brutality, the occasional cases of prisoner abuse, not to mention what our military has done in Iraq and Afghanistan. But then again, there is no such tradition of respecting the rights of individuals at all in Iraq. Recently, the former prime minister said that abuses of citizens under the present Iraqi government are just about as bad as they were under Saddam Hussein. It requires extraordinary restraint for people in authority not to abuse their authority, especially when they believe they are right and the person abused is wrong.

Democracy Will Be Defeated in Iraq

It took several centuries for the ideas of freedom to take root in the United Kingdom and its offspring, which includes us. These are not ideas and traditions that can be forced on people. It's true that everyone longs to be free—free to do as he or she pleases without regard for the rights of anyone else.

The president has bought into the neoconservative idea that we can spread democracy in the Middle East and now appears to believe he's God's man doing God's will. That's part of the tragedy of human history—people with good intentions doing bad things. As long as he defines victory as a permanently free and democratic Iraq, then all he will ever know is defeat.

The United States
Is Not Advocating
Genuine Democracy

Ghali Hassan

Ghali Hassan is a contributing editor to Global Research, a news and analysis Web site run by the Centre for Research on Globalization, a Canadian organization of writers, researchers, and activists.

The *Washington Post*, report[ed in 2005] that President George W. Bush has begun meeting prominent 'foreign dissidents' in an attempt to highlight 'human rights' abuses committed around the world. Dissidents from Venezuela, North Korea, Russia and Belarus have all recently met with Mr. Bush or Secretary of State Condoleezza Rice.

Some Dissidents Exluded

Incidentally, the *Washington Post* also reports that no such meetings took place with dissidents from the US' closest allies such as Uzbekistan, Pakistan, Egypt and Saudi Arabia. All four are the best example of brutal and undemocratic regimes with the worst human rights records in the world.

Let's briefly describe the four countries that President Bush considers unworthy [of] meeting their dissidents. In Uzbekistan where President Islam Karimov rules with an iron fist dissidents are tortured to death and anti-government protesters are killed *en masse* by Karimov's security forces. In Pakistan there have been no elections since General Pervez Musharraf took power by coup d'état. He immediately declared himself the 'Chief Executive' of Pakistan, [and] jailed and exiled every dissident in his way. Egypt is not much different. President Hosni Mubarak took over some 25 years ago and has been a client of the US since. His prison cells and torture chambers are filled with dissidents. The regime of Mubarak is the second largest recipient of US aid after Israel. Saudi Arabia, the US' most trusted ally, is a totalitarian monarchy. In addition, Uzbekistan, Pakistan, Egypt, and Saudi Arabia are Washington destinations for torture of kidnapped citizens accused of alleged "terrorism". Furthermore, these despots are welcomed in Washington and London as guests of honour, and their policies are conducted with the blessings and approvals of Washington and London.

The recent US fanfare about democracy rising in the Middle East is a phantom democracy.

By contrast, Venezuela is very high on Mr. Bush's list of "regime change", and President Hugo Chávez is not likely to receive an invitation to the White House soon. The current Venezuelan government of President Chávez is the most legitimate and democratically elected government in the world. President Chávez was democratically elected in 1998. He has since been re-elected in 2000 and had his presidency reconfirmed in a referendum in August 2004. His current approval rating—an outcome of his popular socio-economic reforms—at 70.5 per cent, but the US insists that Chávez is a threat to democracy. The Bush administration is also involved in propaganda war and military coup to remove President Chávez from office. Venezuela of President Chavez is not as lucky as Uzbekistan, Egypt or Saudi Arabia to be included in US phantom democracy. This example of popular democracy in Venezuela is the form of democracy that the US most feared in developing countries.

Phantom Democracy in the Middle East

The recent US fanfare about democracy rising in the Middle East is a phantom democracy. Saudi Arabia, Mr. Bush tells us, is reforming its decades-long despotic tyranny and corruption, by introducing a male-only 'democracy', and allowing women to obtain driver's licences. The reality is that half of the population (women) were barred from participation in this male-only democracy. And only half of the seats were allowed to be contested and the other half were reserved. In Kuwait and the other Gulf States, the Emirs and Sheikhs select their oppositions. In Egypt, Hosni Mubarak has already barred the Muslim Brotherhood Party [a radical Islamist religious movement] and he will choose an opposition to participate in [the next] elections. In fact President Mubarak is grooming his son for the presidency. It is not democracy; it is a farce.

Any constitutional law book defines democracy as "an internal organisation of the state in which the source and exercise of political power lie with the people, enabling the governed to govern in turn through their elected representatives". However, the people have always been misled and only allowed to watch as spectators, not participants.

The US is never shy to lend [a] hand to brutal dictators.

U.S. Opposition to Genuine Democracy

In his *Essays on Democracy Promotion*, Thomas Carothers, director of the Democracy and Rule of Law Project at the Carnegie Endowment Program for International Peace, and a former State Department official in the [Ronald] Reagan administration, writes; "Where democracy appears to fit in well with US security and economic interests, the United States promotes democracy, [but] where democracy clashes with other significant interests, it is downplayed or even ignored". The history of the past sixty years or so shows that the US has always favoured dictatorial regimes to serve its own interests at the expense of human rights and democracy. For decades the US has supported and encouraged Israel's terror and oppression against the Palestinian people.

When it comes to genuine democracy, the US is enemy number one of democratic principles and international law. In 1953, the US intelligence agents, the CIA, engineered a military coup that toppled Iran's popularly elected Prime Minister Mohammad Mossadegh and replaced him with the three decades-long vicious dictatorial regime of Shah Reza Behlavi. The recent elections in Iran were more transparent and superior democratic processes than the 30 January [2005] US-staged elections in Iraq or the last two US elections [in 2000 and 2004]. However, the US and Western media continue to attack Iran.

U.S. Support for Dictators

The US is never shy to lend [a] hand to brutal dictators. On September 11, 1973, [in Chile] General Augusto Pinochet, with tacit support from the CIA led a violent military [coup] and overthrew the democratically elected Popular Unity government of Salvador Allende. Because of the CIA covert intervention in Chile, and the repressive character of General Pinochet's rule, the coup became the most notorious military takeover in the annals of Latin American history. Thousands of Chilean dissidents have been murdered or disappeared during the military rule of Augusto Pinochet.

On 29 February 2004, just a year after the invasion of Iraq, the US, backed by Canada and France, orchestrated a get together coup d'état against the popular government of President Jean-Bertrand Aristide of Haiti. Deliberately ignored by Western media, a democratically elected government was replaced by [an] unelected, repressive and murderous "Interim Government" which committed hundreds of political killings and more than 700 summary executions (without charges) of political prisoners.

Democracy as a Cover for War in Iraq

From the Middle East to Latin America, the US administrations play the "democracy" card and overtly or covertly support dictators and military dominated regimes that systematically repress and terrorise the local population. The US "promotion of democracy" is not against the *status quo* of dictators, but it is designed for domestic consumption in order to deceive the public that the US is an "honest broker" interested in "democracy". In other word[s], it is a cover for war and control of people's natural resources, including oil.

It was only after the fabricated pretexts for the war on Iraq had collapsed, the Bush administration and its allies turned to imperialism's most favoured propaganda, "democracy". The pretexts keep changing so often that [they] drew little opposition or protest against this flagrant falsification of history regarding the war on Iraq. The Bush administration continues to tell the world that the invasion of Iraq is to "build democracy" throughout the Middle East, as if democracy is another brick in a wall. One important fact to remember is that had Iraq's Arab neighbours been democratically elected governments (like Turkey), the US and Britain wouldn't have unilaterally mounted an illegal invasion into Iraq and committed the kind of international war crimes against the Iraqi people.

The US invaded and occupied Iraq because: 1. Iraq was a defenceless nation . . . ; 2. Iraq is a resources-rich and strategically vital nation; and 3. Iraq . . . [could] counter Israel.

Despite the illegality of the war and the enormous war crimes committed against the Iraqi people, many people, particularly Americans, still believe that the war on Iraq was initiated because of Iraq's possession of WMD [weapons of mass destruction] and Iraq's links to "terrorism". It is now established that Iraq had no WMD since 1991 and that Iraq had no link to "terrorism", and posed no threat to the US, Britain and their allies.

The US invaded and occupied Iraq because: 1. Iraq was a defenceless nation, destroyed by 13-years long genocidal sanctions and constant US-British bombing campaigns; 2. Iraq is a resources-rich and strategically vital nation; and 3. Iraq was and could be a formidable counter to Israel's Zionist expansion. Hence, Iraq was the preferred target for the soon to be US president long before the 9/11 attacks on the US. Also by attacking Iraq, the US intended to send a bullying message to other nations.

The US aim in Iraq is to . . . control Iraq's vital resources and rob Iraq of its wealth and sovereignty at the expense of the Iraqi people.

According to recent reports, Bush believes that, no president is [a] "great" president without winning one military aggression in his presidency. In 1999 Bush revealed his personal motivation to use war in order to advance his domestic political ends. When Bush was asked at a New Hampshire primary event in December 1999 about Saddam Hussein, Bush told David Nyhan of the *Boston Globe*: "I'd take 'em [Saddam] out", and, "take out the weapons of mass destruction. . . . I'm surprised he's [Saddam] still there". This comment alone should be taken as an illegal declaration of war against Iraq and violation of the US Constitution. It follows; the invasion and occupation of Iraq had nothing to do with "democracy", "liberation" or the propaganda perpetuated by Western media, the US government and its allies of the "coalition of the willing". Furthermore, the US invaded Iraq despite massive worldwide protests against an illegal war.

The war perpetrated by the Anglo-American axis ha[s] caused the death of hundreds of thousands of innocent Iraqi civilians, destroyed the Iraqi state and the fabric of the Iraqi society. Tens of thousand of innocent Iraqi men, women and children as young as 12 years old are languishing in hundreds of US-run prison camps and subject to unrestrained torture and abuse by US forces. In addition to the violence, the Occupation has brought Iraqis' desperate living conditions—the destruction of Iraq's health care and education systems, ethnic divisions, and a culture of corruption.

Mr. Bush's claim that "democracy is spreading" throughout the Middle East is simply a phantom to justify an illegal war against Iraq and provides a diversion for the war crimes committed against the Iraqi people. Coupled with military occupation, the US is in a process of political penetration under the rubric of "democracy". This involves the promotion of the Iraqi elites—mostly expatriates, including religious groups, criminal elements and corrupt Kurdish warlords—to high offices. It also involves the corruption of Iraqi and Arab media, trade unions, women organisations and other professional associations to serve the interests of US corporations and enhance [a] US imperial agenda.

The US aim in Iraq is to prolong the Occupation, control Iraq's vital resources and rob Iraq of its wealth and sovereignty at the expense of the Iraqi people. The form of "democracy" the US pretends [to be] building in Iraq is a form of colonial dictatorship dressed in fraudulent elections in order to re-colonise Iraq economically. The US strategy in Iraq is to rule Iraq by the proxy of an "Arab façade", serving Washington and Western interests, and suppressing any alternative popular movement that opposes US design. As pointed out earlier, democracy is never part of US imperialist agenda. If it is not so, then the US should let the Iraqi people decide on the presence of the Occupation forces. If the US is serious about the "spread of democracy" the US must accept the outcome of free and fair elections.

The January 2005 elections were illegitimate and flawed, because Iraq was and continues to be under foreign military occupation. The Iraqi people were deceived [in]to believ[ing] that they were voting to end the Occupation. Although the

US-preferred candidate (Iyad Allawi) lost, the elections [were] still won by those groups who supported the invasion and occupation. Immediately after the elections, the first act of treason the new "government" committed is to extend the presence of the Occupation forces in Iraq, and escalate the violence against the Iraqi people. The London-based Arabic newspaper, *Al-Hayat*, reported . . . that one-third of the members of Iraq's 275 National Assembly have asked for a timetable for the withdrawal of foreign troops from Iraq, accusing the Assembly itself of not caring "about the demands of millions of Iraqis".

Democracy in Iraq Will Fail

Finally, the US strategy is doomed to fail in Iraq. Historically, Iraq is an anti-imperialism ground. The Iraqi people are politically very engaged and educated. It is almost near impossible for a pro-Occupation, pro-US policy regime to survive in Iraq. All Iraqis are united for an immediate withdrawal of foreign troops and end to the Occupation. They have [had] enough of US-perpetrated violence.

People around the world know that the American form of 'democracy' has not benefited the masses. It is an old imperialist tormentor. The invasion and occupation of Iraq have exposed the true nature of this imperialist tormentor. It is the duty of decent men and women not to remain silent and encourage the tormentor to continue tormenting the Iraqi people. Those who committed war crimes and crimes of deception should be held accountable for their actions.

CHAPTER 4

How Should Industrialized Nations Aid the Developing World?

Chapter Preface

In just the last few decades, the world has witnessed a technological revolution that has produced computers, the Internet, mobile phones, and a multitude of other new technologies that have propelled us into what is being called the "Information Age." Many people have predicted that these modern information and communication technologies (ICT) could bring the citizens of the world together, make governments more accountable, improve education levels, help business and commerce, and spread democracy and prosperity around the world. Although the developed world today takes ICT for granted, these new inventions are much less available in developing nations. Older technologies such as radio, television, and print media have slowly spread to many underdeveloped areas, bringing news and information to some of the most remote places on the globe, yet many of the world's poor have never made a phone call, and most developing nations lack access to newer forms of ICT.

Experts say that making technology available to the developing world is an important part of helping poor countries reach goals such as reducing poverty, combating disease, and providing education and opportunity to their populations. The Internet, for example, can be used by developing nations as a classroom to bring education to remote locations where schools or specialized training are not available. Similarly, developing nations can set up online health networks to allow doctors to conduct virtual meetings with patients, to provide a means for health care workers to consult with each other, and to provide medical training and education to citizens. Some countries, too, have set up mobile phone exchanges in areas where landlines do not exist to enable people to better communicate with each other. Other examples of ICT aiding development include the use of email and the Internet to distribute political information and foster civil awareness, and the use of cell phones to allow rural farmers to obtain market prices and sell their goods to the outside world.

In the last decade, a few developing countries have begun to experience rapid growth of some new technologies, particularly the Internet and mobile phones. According to a March 2006 report by Britain's Parliamentary Office of Science and Technology, telephone access (including both mobile and landline) in the developing world increased from 2 percent in 1991 to 31 percent in 2004, while Internet usages jumped from a mere 0.03 percent of developing country inhabitants in 1994 to 6.7 percent in 2004. China, for example, has seen a huge growth spurt in Internet usage just in the last few years, with the number of Chinese Internet subscribers increasing from 33 million in 2001 to 94 million in 2004.

However, the gap between those who have access to ICT and those who don't—often called the "digital divide"—is still quite wide, both between developed and undeveloped countries and within developing countries. Indeed, less than 5 percent of computers connected to the Internet, according to the Global Philanthropy Partnership, are in developing nations. Developed nations such as the United States, Canada and Japan, and countries in Europe have the best access to ICT, while those with the poorest ICT access tend to be sub-Saharan African countries.

Even in those developing countries where computers and other new technologies are becoming available, the poorest citizens generally lack access to ICT because of cost, an absence of ICT infrastructure, or an inability to use technology due to educational deficiencies such as illiteracy or language barriers. People living on a dollar or two a day simply cannot afford computers that cost hundreds of dollars, and even if they could, they may not be able to use them if they cannot read, write, type or access electricity. In India, for example, a developing country with strong economic growth and many new computer users, most of those who use the Internet come from a relatively wealthy, English-speaking minority of the population, while the majority of Indians remain very poor and without access to any modern technology, even telephones.

A variety of strategies are being used to bring ICT to the developing world. Sometimes technology industries have sought to create larger markets for their products by promoting usage in developing areas. In other cases, the technological advances themselves create product demand; the mobile phone and other wireless technologies, for example, are becoming important in remote, rural areas where land connections are not possible or profitable. Governments of developed nations and nongovernmental organizations have also provided aid to help bring ICT to underdeveloped countries.

The issue of ICT and developing countries, however, is a controversial one. Although many people think that ICT is essential to economic development and that everyone should have access to the Internet in order to participate in the world's new information society, others question whether it is wise to spend precious development resources on expensive technologies when many people still lack such basic needs as food, clean water, adequate housing, health care, and education. As some experts have pointed out, for the cost of a computer, a whole school could be built in many developing countries. The answer to this dilemma for many policy makers is that ICT can sometimes help developing countries to achieve development goals, but it should not be given priority or allowed to be a diversion from those goals. As Microsoft founder Bill Gates has said, "PCs and technology can often be part of the solution, [but] we need to remember to put technology in the service of humanity." The authors in this chapter discuss various other ideas for aiding the developing world.

Developed Nations Must Increase Foreign Aid to Help End World Poverty

Silicon Jack

Silicon Jack is the name used by Jack Epstein, a journalist who has written about Latin America for many years. He currently writes for Latin Trade, *a Latin American business magazine.*

In the aftermath of [the December 2004] devastating earthquake and tidal wave [in Indonesia, Thailand, and surrounding areas], rich nations admirably rushed to help the victims. It was a classic response that painfully contrasted with the relative paucity of adequate and sustained efforts to help people who live in extreme poverty in other countries.

The contrast was so sharp that prominent U.S. economist Jeffrey Sachs said: "The world continues to overlook the silent tsunamis" referring to the millions who die annually from preventable diseases. Consider these statistics: Nearly 11 million children die annually before their fifth birthday from such diseases as diarrhea and pneumonia; 2 million to 3 million people die annually from malaria; 500,000 women die each year giving birth, the equivalent of an Asian tsunami every four months; 3 million die annually from AIDS, equivalent to an Asian tsunami every three weeks.

The Need for Aid

Early [in 2005], the United Nations [U.N.] announced a three-year study on global poverty headed by Sachs that's a blueprint for halving extreme poverty, defined as living on US$1 a day or less, by 2015. The 3,000-page assessment by 265 experts is straightforward—rich countries must increase development aid to poor countries so they can finance clean water projects, sanitation, food, medicine, housing and school lunches.

[The gap between rich and poor in developing countries] could narrow if rich countries raised development aid to $195 billion by 2015.

There are 221 million poor people in Latin America—44% of the total population—of which 97 million live in extreme poverty, according to the U.N. Economic Commission for Latin America and the Caribbean. In a speech [in 2005] to the Organization of American States, former U.S. President Jimmy Carter said millions of Latin Americans could turn to "radical and destructive" behavior unless their sub-standard living conditions improve. "The greatest challenge of our time is the growing gap between the rich and poor," he said.

That gap could narrow if rich countries raised development aid to $195 billion by 2015, a figure the U.N. projects, from $58 billion a year in 2004. The world's current military budget is an estimated $900 billion. Increasing development aid would also meet U.N. Millennium Development goals set in 2000 and endorsed by 190 member nations to not only halve extreme poverty within 15 years but end hunger, achieve universal primary education, promote gender equality, reduce child and maternal mortality and reverse the spread of diseases such as malaria and AIDS.

To meet U.N. objectives, rich nations agreed to increase foreign aid to 0.7 percent of their gross national incomes by 2015. To date, only Sweden, Norway, Denmark, the Netherlands and Luxembourg have complied. The United States, with the world's largest economy at $12 trillion, gives 15 one-hundredths of 1% (not including private aid), dead last among major donor nations. In his State of the Union address in

February [2005], U.S. President George W. Bush made no mention of world poverty or foreign aid. "The world is crying out for leadership on this issue. If the U.S. leads, other countries will come on board," David Morrison, chairman of the board of Directors of NetAid, a philanthropic organization founded by the Silicon Valley's Cisco Systems and the United Nations Development Program, told me.

Preoccupied with Security

Poor countries are ultimately responsible for their own development, and much aid money has been historically lost to corruption. And, yes, throwing money at problems is not always the answer. But the U.N. report mandates poor nations to do their part by developing a national plan to end poverty, combat corruption and demonstrate that they can use aid effectively. The U.N. report will likely force global poverty to the top of the agenda, along with security, at the G-8 meeting in July [2005]. [In 2004], [former] World Bank President James Wolfensohn said the developed world's interest in global poverty is "near a low point" since it has "become preoccupied with security." Rising crime and global terrorism are certainly real threats, but crime and terrorism feed on poverty.

If rich countries keep their promise, billions of people will join the global economy, more than 500 million people will be lifted out of extreme poverty, millions will avoid death from "silent tsunamis," and countries that would have descended into political chaos will stabilize. This is not a utopian idea but a ticket to a better and a safer world. The question is not whether rich countries can afford it. These are trivial sums, 50 cents of every $100 of income. The question is whether they can afford not to.

Foreign Aid Alone Will Not Help Developing Countries Eliminate Poverty

Raghuram Rajan

Raghuram Rajan is the economic counselor and director of research at the International Monetary Fund.

Now that developed countries and international financial institutions have committed themselves to writing off the debt of highly indebted poor countries, the challenge will be to convert these resources into actual growth and faster progress toward the Millennium Development Goals [set by the United Nations for helping developing countries by 2015]. While for some it may seem that the war against poverty can be won simply by getting rich countries to provide more debt relief and aid, the view of experts—including those behind recent reports by the U.K. [United Kingdom] Commission for Africa and the Millennium Project—is that this is just one of the necessary ingredients. It's early days yet in the campaign to make poverty history. If it's to succeed, we have to recognize the failures of the past as well as be open-minded about the solutions for the future. And the first thing to recognize is the chequered history of aid.

Aid and Economic Growth

The best way to get the poor in low-income countries out of poverty is to strengthen economic growth in those countries. To the layperson, this may mean just sending these countries more aid. Yet one point about which there is general agree-

Raghuram Rajan, "Aid and Growth: The Policy Challenge: We Need More Than Aid to Break the Cycle of Poverty," *Finance & Development*, vol. 42, no. 4, December 2005, pp. 53–55. Copyright © 2005 International Monetary Fund. Republished with permission of International Monetary Fund, conveyed through Copyright Clearance Center, Inc.

ment among economists is that there is little evidence of a robust unconditional effect of aid on growth. . . . Does this mean that aid can't, in any circumstances, boost growth? Of course not! The layperson's thinking does, of course, have some significant basis. Poor countries are short of resources and ought to be able to put aid inflows to good use. There are case studies of countries that have grown using aid, and specific aid projects that have helped the poor enormously. What we economists haven't identified is a reliable set of economic circumstances in which we can say that aid has helped countries grow. And this isn't for want of trying.

For example, an influential study suggested that aid leads to growth, but only in countries that have good governance. This certainly seemed a very reasonable conclusion—a necessary condition for aid to help growth is obviously that aid receipts shouldn't be spirited away to [unscrupulous leaders'] Swiss bank accounts. Unfortunately, however, it doesn't seem to be a sufficient condition for aid to help growth, since follow-up studies suggest the finding isn't robust. It would appear that other levers are needed in addition to reasonable governance for aid to be effective. . . .

Micro-interventions or programs . . . might be very helpful, say, in furthering education and health, which undoubtedly lead to growth.

It should, however, be of concern to the layperson that the best example we have of aid working systematically for a group of countries is the Marshall Plan, whereby the ravaged countries of postwar Western Europe were returned to the ranks of the rich. The reason it worked so well might be that these countries' institutions, including the education of their people, were probably then capable of sustaining much higher per capita GDP [gross domestic product] than their postwar low. Perhaps this is why one might see a country emerging from conflict experience a substantial period of catch-up growth, when aid is very effective—Mozambique or Uganda might be more recent examples. Nevertheless, it should be sobering that the canonical recent example of a country clawing itself out of poverty into the ranks of the rich is Korea. Korea was indeed ravaged by war, but its spectacular growth started approximately when aid inflows tapered off.

A Better Way: Micro-Intervention

According to some, there is a better way—to focus on what we know works. Specifically, funding should support micro-interventions or programs, validated through evaluations and experimentation, that might be very helpful, say, in furthering education and health care, which undoubtedly lead to growth. Here, we have learned a lot from work by Abhijit Banerjee of the Massachusetts Institute of Technology, Michael Kremer at Harvard, and their students, as well as from the World Bank, including its World Development Report 2004.

We know that providing services to the poor isn't just about money. One can build spanking new schools and pay teachers a good wage, yet they may not come in to teach. One can provide free drugs to the hospitals, intended for the poor, but the druggist may simply sell them on the black market. This isn't to say that schools and hospitals aren't necessary, but bricks and mortar are often the easy part. Policymakers also need to create the right incentives for the service provider and the poor client, as well as the right allocation of power and information between them to ensure that reasonable quality services are provided. And we know that the law of unintended consequences is always at work. This means that few programs ever operate as the designers intended, so we need abundant experimentation, frequent monitoring and evaluation, and a sharing of best practices so that these targeted interventions can have their intended effect.

Avoiding Dutch Disease

Unfortunately, I'm not sure that even if each micro-intervention works well by itself, they will all work well together. Interventions could affect each other and get in each other's way or vie for the same resources. They could also have adverse spillover effects on the rest of the economy.

Investments in health and education—which create a population that not only lives a better life but also sees opportunities in growth and competition—ought to be encouraged.

The last isn't just a possibility. Suppose a lot of aid flows in to support interventions in education, health care, and other social services. The recipient country quickly hires many educated workers as teachers, clerks, nurses, foremen (to build the schools), engineers, and government and aid administrators. Because well educated people will be in high demand, their wages will tend to rise and may well go up rapidly. In turn, factories will have to escalate the wages they pay to managers, engineers, and supervisors. Now factories that produce for the domestic market and don't face competition can pass on their higher costs. But factories that export can't, so they will cut down on operations and even start shutting down. This is one example of a phenomenon called Dutch disease, which makes aid recipients less competitive. . . . In countries that received more aid in the 1980s and 1990s, the export-oriented, labor-intensive industries not only grew more slowly than other industries—suggesting that aid did in fact create Dutch disease—but the manufacturing sector as a whole also grew more slowly. Again it's sobering to think that by constraining the growth of manufacturing, aid inflows may have prevented recipient countries from taking the path to growth followed first by the East Asian tigers [nations with aggressive economies] and now by China.

That said, Dutch disease is not a terminal condition. It can be mitigated through sensible policies. But to do so, one must first acknowledge its existence and its pernicious effects. The same goes for other possible diseases caused by aid.

There Is Hope

To ignore the past, or to read only rosy lessons from it, is to condemn oneself to relive it. While it would be churlish to deny that many poor countries have made tremendous progress in creating the conditions for sustained growth, it doesn't serve the citizens of poor countries either if we say that all the problems of the past are well and truly in the past. While no one has the "magic bullet" for growth, there are some things that do seem important. These include sensible macroeconomic management, with fiscal discipline, moderate inflation, and a reasonably competitive exchange rate; laws and policies that create an environment conducive to private sector activity with low transaction costs; and a economy open for international trade. In addition, investments in health and education—which create a population that not only lives a better life but also sees opportunities in growth and competition—ought to be encouraged.

One way rich countries and international financial institutions can help is by making policies that broadly meet these requirements an essential condition for aid. They should, however, resist micromanaging and overlaying broad economic conditionality with too many detailed economic prescriptions, or with social and political conditionality. Once a country has the necessary broad environment in place, it should have the freedom to chart its own path. After all, the failure of past grand theories of growth should make us wary of becoming overly prescriptive.

Rich countries can also help by reducing the impediments they place in the way of poor country exports, and by coaxing these countries to lower their own trade barriers, including barriers to other poor countries. They can spend more to foster research on drugs and agricultural technologies that would benefit the poorest countries. They can be more active in ensuring that their companies and officials don't grease the wheels of corruption in poor countries. And they should never hesitate to give humanitarian aid in the face of a disaster.

[Should] the world . . . hesitate to give humanitarian aid? Absolutely not! But the form of the aid matters.

Let us draw hope from the willingness of the outside world to provide more, and better, aid. Ultimately, though, poor countries hold their future in their own hands. It's only through their own will and actions that the good intentions of the outside world can be used to truly make poverty history.

How About Humanitarian Aid?

Does this cautious approach toward aid in general mean that the world should hesitate to give humanitarian aid? Absolutely not! But the form of the aid matters. In the midst of a humanitarian disaster, one should concentrate on getting enough relief in kind to the affected area if local production is typically not possible (for example, because the failure of local crops is the proximate cause of the humanitarian disaster). Aid sent in the form of cash may, however, be better if supplies are available but the distressed population doesn't have the buying power. Aid could then create more local jobs. Also, when the immediate emergency is over, donors should be careful that additional aid doesn't hamper incentives for local production—that, for example, donated secondhand clothes don't kill the business of local tailors.

And every so often, donors are confronted with the Good Samaritan's dilemma. An uncaring local government siphons off a fraction of the humanitarian aid in return for allowing the aid to get through to the starving people. While the aid reduces the immediate suffering of the people, it also entrenches the government, perpetuating the people's long-term suffering. There are no easy solutions to this dilemma.

Cancellation of Developing Countries' Debts Is Necessary to Cut Global Poverty

Sarah Anderson

Sarah Anderson is the director of the Global Economy Project of the Institute for Policy Studies, a progressive think tank.

Many Americans can relate to the feeling of drowning in debt. Credit card companies have pushed high-interest plastic on young people to the point where 18–24-year-olds now spend an average of one third of their income on debt payments. Predatory lenders take advantage of relatively high unemployment among low-income African-Americans and Latinos to push loans at usury rates. And about 1.5 million Americans file for personal bankruptcy per year—half of them because they can't pay their medical bills.

If you fell into a debt hole because you couldn't find decent work, got sick, or were snookered by an irresponsible lender, you would likely be angry—and justifiably. But imagine for a minute how you might feel if you weren't even the one who took out the loans that were making your life hard? What if it was your government? And what if the government that took out the loans was not elected by the people but took power by force? And what if the loans were spent not on education or other productive investments, but instead were wasted on palaces or boondoggle projects? What if the debts existed before you were even born?

These are the types of debts that are dragging down many of the most impoverished people in the world. During the 1960s and 1970s, rich country lenders encouraged developing country governments, including many brutal dictatorships, to take on large debts that have since snowballed to unmanageable levels. This report focuses on 77 countries, which are referred to throughout this report as "heavily indebted countries," that have a combined total debt burden of $1.25 trillion. They include 67 countries that have been identified as ones that need immediate debt cancellation in order to have any hope of achieving the Millennium Development Goals—targets set by the United States and most other countries through the United Nations [UN] to cut extreme poverty in half and achieve other social goals by the year 2015. These 67 impoverished countries have a combined external debt of $819 billion.

Many governments, particularly in Africa, spend more money per year servicing their debts than they do on health or education for their people.

Also included in the sample are 10 countries widely recognized as ones strapped with debts accumulated under dictatorships (often called 'odious' debts). These countries' debts total $432 billion. The combined debt burdens of the 77 countries in our sample amount to about half of the $2.5 trillion owed by all 153 developing countries in the world.

Is All Debt Bad?

As any Mom & Pop [small business] knows, borrowing is often an unavoidable part of running a successful business. Most parents understand the long-term value of college loans. Impoverished countries also need and should have access to credit for productive investments. But the current reality is that new loans are too often used merely to help pay off old loans, many of which were illegitimate in the first place. On average, low-income countries spend about $100 million per day just to pay the interest on these loans. This means that many governments, particularly in Africa, spend more money per year servicing their debts than they do on health or education for their people.

The burden of these debts is not just on the backs of people in the Global South [of the equator, site of most of the world's developing nations]. Although the impacts there are much more direct and life-threatening, they can be felt in our own country [the United States] as well. . . . These problems come back to strike us in our own country in five major ways:

1. Lost Jobs and Markets

2. International Health Undermined

3. Global Warming

4. Global Insecurity

5. Immigration Pressures

There will always be some corrupt leaders who prefer to use the proceeds [of aid] to buy weapons or build palaces rather than improving their people's lives.

Most Americans know intuitively that today's world is an interconnected place. It is our hope that this report may help raise awareness of how much our welfare and the welfare of people in impoverished countries are linked. Canceling developing country debts is not only the moral and just thing to do. It is also in our interest.

Does Debt Cancellation Work?

Heavy debts are only one obstacle to progress in the Global South. Major changes are also needed in the international financial institutions that govern the global economy and in the international trade rules that favor global corporations over the rest of us. And at home and abroad, efforts to promote social goals through debt cancellation and other types of assistance will be vastly more effective if combined with good governance. We urge readers to consider some of the many well-thought-through proposals for change and become engaged in seeking solutions to these problems.

Just as debt is not the root of all problems, neither is debt cancellation a panacea. There will always be some corrupt leaders who prefer to use the proceeds to buy weapons or build palaces rather than improving their people's lives. But even the small amount of debt relief given so far has led to remarkable results. For example:

- more than doubling school enrollment in Uganda,

- eliminating fees to allow 1.6 million Tanzanian children to return to school,

- a 50% increase in education and health spending in 10 African countries,

- programs that have successfully stabilized HIV rates in Burkina Faso, and

- plans to add more than 4,500 teachers and 800 medical personnel in Zambia.

In 2005, . . . rich countries agreed to cancel the debts of 18 developing countries, . . . [but this] leaves out many countries that need full cancellation now.

Further debt cancellation would give impoverished country governments a better chance of reducing inequality and protecting the environment in their countries.

A Critical Moment for Debt Cancellation

As [author] Susan George wrote . . . [in her 1992 book] *Debt Boomerang*, "Perhaps if enough people in the North realize that the Third World debt crisis is their crisis as well, they will insist on radically different policies. They will speak out and will seek to join with similar forces in the South." Since that time, many people have spoken out, and there have been positive changes. In 2005, the Group of Eight (G8) rich countries agreed to cancel the debts of 18 developing countries. This plan set an important precedent, but [it] is flawed because it comes with onerous conditions and leaves out many countries that need full cancellation now. Building on this momentum is critical. The [George W.] Bush Administration already committed to do more when it endorsed the 2000 UN Millennium Development Goals, which include a pledge to cut global poverty in half by 2015 through debt relief and other assistance. If these goals are to be reached, we must amplify our calls now for a better and broader plan for debt cancellation. . . .

Why Is the Recent Debt Deal Not Enough?

Many Countries Excluded: The deal applies only to 18 countries that have completed the Heavily Indebted Poor Countries (HIPC) Initiative of the World Bank and IMF [International Monetary Fund]. This program was started in 1996 to reduce the debts of countries that adopt economic reforms approved by the Bank and Fund. At least 44 more countries need immediate debt cancellation in order to achieve the UN Millennium Development Goals. At least 10 more countries that are burdened by "dictator debt" should be considered for debt relief.

Debts Remaining: Even the 18 countries that are included in the deal will still be saddled with significant debts. The deal applies only to debts owed to the World Bank, IMF, and African Development Fund. Thus, many of the 18 countries owe significant sums to other institutions, including $403.85 million to the African Development Bank alone.

More Hoops: It is not yet clear whether new conditions will be imposed on the countries in line to benefit from the deal. . . . World Bank and IMF conditions have typically included onerous austerity measures to slash government spending, including for essential services; reforms that undermine worker protections; and privatization of government enterprises, including basic services like water, which has often resulted in mass layoffs and reduced access to services for the poor.

The time is now to push the U.S. government to support an improved debt plan without onerous conditions that covers more countries.

Some Concrete Steps

Education: As the outpouring of support for victims of the 2004 tsunami [in the Indian Ocean] and other disaster shows, there is widespread desire in the United States to lift up those in need around the world. Polls also show that the majority of Americans disapprove of the job their government is doing to improve the lives of people living in impoverished countries. But while there may be widespread interest in improving U.S. policies towards the developing world, there is little understanding about how to do it. We need to build on the great educational work that has been done over the past two decades on debt to reach new audiences.

- IPS [Institute for Policy Studies] is producing accessible educational tools based on the "Debt Boomerang" research. . . .

- [Many nongovernmental] groups . . . can provide useful materials and other assistance, including helping to set up a workshop or town hall meeting featuring speakers from heavily indebted countries.

- The mainstream media needs to be pushed to become a better source of information about the Global South and measures like debt cancellation that can lead to positive change. Take every opportunity to write letters to the editor and urge journalists to do more and better reporting of these issues.

Engage Policymakers: U.S. government holds more power than any other to make debt cancellation for impoverished countries a reality. It holds veto power over decisions within the World Bank and IMF and could use its superpower status to influence other rich country governments. And while we urge the President to do the right thing, we should also be encouraging elected officials at all levels to add their voices to the global calls for debt cancellation.

- IPS's Cities for Progress project is working with other allied organizations to mobilize community-based activists and local elected officials to support City Council resolutions in support of debt cancellation and the Millennium Development Goals. These local-level initiatives can be leveraged to influence power at the national level. . . .

- The U.S. Congress holds tremendous potential power to influence the World Bank and IMF through its budget authority to set U.S. government financial contributions to these institutions. Jubilee USA Network and other groups are leading efforts to engage members of the U.S. Congress to play a stronger role in the debt debate.

- Through groups like Jubilee's international networks and the Global Call to Action on Poverty you can increase pressure on global leaders in support of debt cancellations. . . .

The Right Thing to Do

Calling for debt cancellation is a matter of solidarity with those in impoverished countries as well as the interest of people in the United States. . . .

Debt cancellation is no magic panacea. We cannot lose sight of other factors that have crippled impoverished countries' abilities to ensure that their people can meet basic needs and live in a stable environment. At the same time, we must recognize that we cannot transform the world overnight. One thing we can do, though, is build on the momentum generated by people across the globe to achieve this one concrete step towards a more equitable and peaceful world. If the political will were there, debt cancellation for all impoverished countries could happen next week.

We can make it happen. It's the right thing to do, and it's in our interest.

Agricultural Trade Reform Is the Key to Reducing World Poverty

The World Bank

The World Bank is a global development institution owned by 184 member countries that provides low-interest loans, interest-free credit, and grants to developing countries for education, health, infrastructure, communications, and many other purposes.

With almost 70 percent of the poor people in developing countries living in rural areas, agricultural sector reform—in particular global trade liberalization—will be crucial in giving them opportunities for better lives, according to a new World Bank report released [January 10, 2005].

The report, *Global Agricultural Trade and Developing Countries*, edited by M. Ataman Aksoy and John C. Beghin, notes that ... agricultural protection continues to be among the most contentious issues in global trade negotiations. High protection of agriculture in industrial countries was the main cause of the breakdown of the Cancún Ministerial Meetings [trade talks held in Cancún, Mexico] in 2003, and remains among the key outstanding issues in the Doha Round of global trade negotiation [a series of global trade talks aimed at helping developing nations].

Developing countries are investing to increase their agricultural productivity, but these gains will not be fully translated into poverty reduction unless industrial and some middle-income countries reduce agricultural trade protection, the report says. In the absence of reduced protection in these countries, increased productivity in agriculture will instead

The World Bank, "Agricultural Trade Reform Key to Reducing Poverty," January 10, 2005. http://usinfo.state.gov.

give rise to overproduction and price declines for many commodities, undermining competitive poor countries' efforts to expand exports and rural incomes. It also increases pressure for greater protection globally.

Unequal Trade Reform

Identifying superior policy options is not difficult, the report states, but the feasibility of reform depends on the power of vested interests, and the ability of governments to identify efficient tradeoffs among multiple goals—such as food security, income transfers, and expansion of higher-value products in agriculture. "Manufacturing protection has declined worldwide following substantial reforms of trade policies, especially in developing countries. Yet many industrial and developing countries still protect agriculture at high levels, which is hitting the world's poor the hardest," said François Bourguignon, the World Bank's Senior Vice President and Chief Economist. "Growth in agriculture has a disproportionately positive effect on poverty reduction, because more than half the population in developing countries lives in rural areas, and poverty is highest in rural areas. This report clearly shows the need for coordinated, global trade reforms if we are to help the rural poor." . . .

While protection remains high in industrial countries, many developing countries have liberalized their agricultural sectors. Average agricultural tariffs, the main source of protection in developing countries, declined from 30 percent to 18 percent during the 1990s but are still higher than manufacturing tariffs. In addition, many of these countries eliminated other forms of import restrictions, abandoning multiple exchange rate systems that penalized agriculture, and eliminating almost all export taxes. However, "reactive protection" in response to industrial-country support to agricultural producers began to increase in many middle-income countries, especially in food products.

The report notes that low-income countries have seen increased agricultural trade surpluses in their trade with both middle-income developing countries and industrial countries. But low-income developing countries now export more to middle-income countries than they do to the European Union, their largest export market in the early 1980s, and the agricultural trade surpluses of middle-income countries have diminished. Among industrial countries, Japan has the largest agricultural trade deficit (almost $50 billion in 2000–01); the European Union, once the largest net buyer of agricultural commodities, has seen its deficits decline; and NAFTA [North American Free Trade Agreement, a trade agreement between the United States, Mexico, and Canada] members' trade surplus with the rest of the world has shrunk considerably.

[Trade] reform would reduce rural poverty in developing economies ... [because] the agricultural sector is important for income generation in these countries.

Projections in the report indicate that without significant reforms, the agricultural trade surpluses of industrial countries will increase while the developing countries will face increasing agricultural trade deficits, exacerbating rural poverty.

Potential Winners and Losers from Agriculture Trade Reforms

The report identifies both the key policy instruments that distort competition and likely winners and losers from global reforms, including producers, consumers, and taxpayers within and across countries. Knowing who is likely to gain or lose from a given reform is critical for sequencing reforms and putting in place complementary policies, including assistance to reduce the cost of adjustment in noncompetitive sectors.

The report concludes that reform would reduce rural poverty in developing economies, both because, in the aggregate, they have a strong comparative advantage in agriculture and because the agricultural sector is important for income generation in these countries. . . .

Implementation of Reforms Is Critical

How reforms occur will have important consequences for developing countries, the report says, noting that the best approach is coordinated global liberalization of policies. The report illustrates the importance of a multi-commodity [i.e., multiple products] approach to reform, as gains and losses do differ greatly by market. This approach would also allow the countries to trade off gains in some commodities against the losses in others. For example, world sugar price increases alone would offset about half the lost quota rents, or about $450 million, for countries with preferential access. The analysis shows that losses in rents would be much less than is commonly expected, as high production costs eat up much of the potential benefit from preferential access to the high-price markets.

Consumers in highly-protected markets will benefit greatly from trade liberalization as domestic (tariff-inclusive) prices fall and product choice expands. Consumers in poor, net-food-importing countries could face higher prices if these markets were not protected before liberalization, because of higher import unit costs. In practice, however, such concerns have often been exaggerated.

For example, dairy consumption in the Middle East and North Africa would be little affected by trade liberalization because, while world prices would rise, high import tariffs would be removed, so that the net impact on dairy consumer prices would be negligible. Similarly, rice prices will decline for consumers in most rice importing developing countries in Asia and Africa.

Commodity-by-Commodity Distortions

The report breaks new ground in providing a comprehensive analysis of individual commodities—sugar, dairy, rice, wheat, groundnuts [peanuts], fruits and vegetables, cotton, seafood and coffee—providing specific examples of how large trade distortions impede trade flows, depress world prices, and discourage market entry or delay exit by noncompetitive producers. These commodity studies also show that reforms will lead to large gains, confirming the results of global models.

The report finds that border barriers are high in most of the commodity markets studied (the exceptions are cotton, coffee, and seafood), including industrial and many developing countries. For example, the global trade-weighted average tariff for all types of rice is 43 percent and reaches 217 percent for Japonica rice. Many Asian countries remain bastions of protectionism in their agricultural and food markets.

Subsidies have similar effects, depressing world prices and inhibiting entry by inducing surplus production by noncompetitive, and often large producers. Cotton subsidies in the United States and European Union, for example, have reached $4.4 billion in a $20 billion market. In dairy and sugar markets, the effects of export subsidies have been smaller than those of tariffs and tariff rate quota schemes, partly because of the export subsidy disciplines introduced in the Uruguay Round Agreement on Agriculture.

Domestic support and protection policies have substantial negative effects on producers in developing countries, because of the sheer size of the subsidies relative to the size of the market. Such large support programs shield non-competitive producers, and penalize efficient producers, often in poor countries.

Fighting Corruption in Developing Nations Is Essential to Promote Economic Development and Reduce Poverty

U.S. Agency for International Development

The U.S. Agency for International Development (USAID) is the principal U. S. agency for extending assistance to countries recovering from disaster, trying to escape poverty, and engaging in democratic reforms.

USAID is a leader in fighting corruption. The Agency's work reduces opportunities and incentives for corruption; supports stronger and more independent judiciaries, legislatures, and oversight bodies; and promotes independent media, civil society, and public education. Yet corruption—the abuse of entrusted authority for private gain—remains a tremendous obstacle to political, social, and economic development, and efforts to reduce it need to be more fully integrated into USAID programs across all sectors.

Anticorruption efforts have tended to focus on what is sometimes the most immediately visible dimension of the problem: administrative corruption—mostly smaller transactions involving mid- and low-level government officials. Anticorruption efforts need to be expanded to better encompass grand corruption—exchanges of resources, access to rents, or other competitive advantages for privileged firms and high-level officials in the executive, judiciary, or legislature, or in political parties. New analytical approaches help illuminate a broader range of assistance strategies and tactics—many already in USAID's portfolio—that can help target the critical problem of corruption in all its manifestations.

USAID, "Anticorruption Strategy," January 2005. www.usaid.gov.

Fighting corruption is emerging as an important U.S. foreign policy objective, and USAID anticorruption programs are expanding. This USAID strategy builds on the Agency's experience and provides an opportunity to further advance its leadership.

Corruption, Development, and U.S. National Security

There is an emerging global consensus that fighting corruption and building good governance are essential for the development of people, markets, and nations. Corruption undermines social cohesion and broad participation in economic and political life by distorting the allocation of resources and the delivery of public services, usually in ways that particularly damage the poor. It also damages prospects for economic growth by reducing foreign direct investment, skewing public investment, encouraging firms to operate in the informal sector, distorting the terms of trade, and weakening the rule of law and protection of property rights. In doing all this, corruption fundamentally weakens the legitimacy and effectiveness of new democracies.

In addition, the current U.S. National Security Strategy underscores that poverty, weak institutions, and corruption can make states vulnerable to terrorist networks and drug cartels, and argues that efforts to address these challenges in developing countries can contribute directly to U.S. national security.

USAID's Role in U.S. Anticorruption Efforts

USAID is cooperating with a broad range of U.S. Government agencies (including the Departments of State, Treasury, Commerce, and Justice), bilateral donors, international organizations, and NGOs [nongovernmental organizations] to address corruption globally. Diplomacy, international law enforcement efforts, and development assistance are complementary and mutually reinforcing dimensions of a global U.S. Government anticorruption effort.

USAID works to reduce opportunities and incentives for corruption through public sector reform and deregulation, support for oversight and watchdog activities, and education of citizens about their roles in preventing corruption. USAID brings about sustainable change by building on its experience in institutional development and through its engagement with national and local governments. The Agency has a special comparative advantage in its experience working outside of government with the private sector, political parties, trade unions, NGOs, universities, professional associations, and others.

USAID Anticorruption Work

The Agency has invested significant resources—$184 million in FY [fiscal year] 2001 and $222 million in FY 2002, according to a 2003 survey, in programs specifically targeting corruption, as well as those broadly aimed at "governance" but with a significant anticorruption dimension. The same survey showed that more than two-thirds of all USAID missions have some programs related to corruption and that most missions are interested in expanding these programs.

Fighting the scourge of corruption is fundamental to advancing U.S. foreign policy interests.

The following broad actions will assist USAID to better address the development challenges posed by corruption:

- *Confront the dual challenges of grand and administrative corruption.* In the past, many USAID anticorruption programs have successfully targeted low-level, or administrative, corruption through bureaucratic and regulatory reform and public education and monitoring. In those countries where corruption is systemic and driven from the highest levels, however, efforts to address administrative corruption must be complemented by efforts to address high-level, or grand, corruption. USAID is developing a new assessment methodology that will provide a more comprehensive framework to analyze the locations, dynamics, and scale of corruption and the balance between grand and administrative corruption. The objective is to ensure that USAID interventions address the varying patterns of corruption; develop innovative strategies to address grand corruption; expand and improve strategies to curtail lower-level, administrative corruption; and develop sectoral and cross-sectoral strategies to reduce corruption and improve governance.

- *Deploy Agency resources strategically to fight corruption.* The Agency must deploy its resources strategically and must allocate a greater proportion of available resources to reducing corruption. Missions and bureaus can leverage resources by incorporating anticorruption components into all sectoral programs affected by corruption (including agriculture, education, energy, and health, in addition to democracy and governance and economic growth); focusing democracy and governance and economic growth resources more explicitly on anticorruption; and increasing the share of funds dedicated to specific anticorruption initiatives. The Agency will develop rapid response capabilities to enable USAID to augment anticorruption efforts quickly when key opportunities arise. The Agency also will explore and respond to requirements presented by the Millennium Challenge Account [a repository for U.S. funds designated for global development].

- *Incorporate anticorruption goals and activities across Agency work.* USAID must pay attention to organizational incentives and structures that support or resist a broadened approach to Agency anticorruption efforts. A comprehensive implementation plan will develop next steps to establish a budget code to track resources devoted to anticorruption; incorporate specific anticorruption goals into mission and bureau strategies and results frameworks; build collaboration by establishing integrated interagency and donor coordination mechanisms; include anticorruption in Agency training, communication, and planning vehicles; and continue and expand Agency leadership on fighting corruption.

- *Build USAID's anticorruption knowledge.* Anticorruption assistance is a relatively new area of practice; thus, the Agency should strive to expand anticorruption knowledge. Evaluating program effectiveness and impact will better enable the Agency to measure and improve the effectiveness of its programs. Establishing an Agency-wide "community of practice" will encourage the collection and dissemination of anticorruption learning. Engaging the Agency in a dialogue on gender and corruption will illuminate important and challenging: issues.

Fundamental to U.S. Interests

Fighting the scourge of corruption is fundamental to advancing U.S. foreign policy interests. Corruption is now seen unequivocally as a major barrier to development, and reducing it a top priority. USAID has made important advances but must expand its approaches to fighting corruption, especially grand corruption; build new knowledge to design better interventions; support countries making real efforts to improve; and be quick to respond to emerging opportunities. Implementation of the actions in this strategy will help USAID make a significant contribution to the fight against corruption.

Redistribution of the World's Wealth Is Necessary to End World Poverty

Sam Pizzigati

Sam Pizzigati is a journalist and editor of Too Much, *an online weekly newsletter on excessive income and wealth published by the Council on International and Public Affairs. He also serves as an associate fellow at the Institute for Policy Studies, a progressive think tank.*

Some people, at year's end, like to spread holiday cheer. The world might do better, suggests a landmark [2006] report from the United Nations [UN] University in Helsinki [Finland], to start spreading wealth. The new study—the first ever to tally, for the entire world, all the major elements of household wealth, everything from financial assets and debts to land, homes, and other tangible property—finds some $125.3 trillion worth of wealth about in the world, as of the year 2000. If that wealth were divided in perfectly equal shares among all the world's 3.7 billion adults, every adult on Earth would hold a net worth of just under $34,000 in U.S. dollars, according to *The World Distribution of Household Wealth* report.

Most Wealth in Few Pockets

In real life, says this report, released by the United Nations University's World Institute for Development Economics Research, half the world's adults hold under one-tenth that modest sum, less than $2,161. The vast bulk of the world's wealth, the study observes, sits "highly concentrated" in the pockets of a relative few. How concentrated? The richest 5 percent of the world's adults—minimum net worth $150,145—hold 70.6 percent of the world's wealth. The richest 1 percent—minimum wealth, $514,512—hold 39.9 percent of the world's wealth all by themselves, 13,000 times more than the entire bottom 10 percent.

The scholars behind the new UN University study base their calculations on a growing body of wealth data that nearly all the world's developed nations—as well as developing giants like India and China—are now collecting. This research has helped heap onto the statistical table "an impressive amount of information on wealth holdings," enough to finally "estimate the world distribution of household wealth." The study's four co-authors—Canadian economist James Davies, Finnish researcher Susanna Sandstrom, New York University economist Edward Wolff, and British economist Anthony Shorrocks—accumulated data for the new UN University study from countries that represent 56 percent of the world's population. They then analyzed these numbers for trends and patterns that allowed to impute wealth distributions for the rest of the world.

Stark Global Inequality

The researchers sliced and diced this collection of statistics by all sorts of yardsticks. They looked at the world's wealth by households, by adults, and by all persons. They used both currency exchange rates and purchasing power equivalents to compare the wealth that sits in different nations. These different calculations resulted in somewhat different numbers. But all the numbers painted the same basic picture, a global portrait of a deeply unequal world. Their new study expresses this inequality in terms both highly technical and readily understandable.

The report, for instance, translates the global distribution of wealth into a common statistical measure called a Gini coefficient, where "0" represents a situation where wealth is divided in total equality and "1" the opposite, a situation where one person owns everything. The higher the fraction in between, the more severe the inequality. The UN University study computes the year 2000 global wealth Gini at 0.892, a level higher than the inequality rate within any individual country. What does this abstract number mean in actual people terms? If you reduced the world's population to 10 people, the study points out, this 0.892 Gini would correspond to a situation where the richest of the 10 people held $1,000 in wealth and the remaining nine a single $1 each.

In the United States, . . . the distribution of wealth runs strikingly top-heavy. The bottom 90 percent of Americans hold just 30.2 percent of U.S. household wealth.

But this stark global inequality, the study's authors take pains to note, does not translate into stark inequality within every nation. Inequality within nations, "even for countries at a similar stage of development," varies enormously across the world.

Japan v. United States

Two similarly "wealthy" nations—the United States and Japan—provide what may be the most dramatic contrast. At first glance, the two seem equally "rich." Americans average, in purchasing power equivalence, a net worth of $143,727. The Japanese average: $124,858. The two countries, together, account for almost two-thirds of the richest 1 percent of adults on the globe, with 37.4 percent of these affluent souls living in the United States and another 26.8 percent in Japan.

But a closer look reveals striking differences. Japan's wealth spreads throughout Japanese society. The 90 percent of Japanese at the bottom of their nation's wealth distribution own 60.7 percent of their nation's wealth. In the United States, by contrast, the distribution of wealth runs strikingly top-heavy.

The bottom 90 percent of Americans own just 30.2 percent of U.S. household wealth, less than half the share the bottom 90 percent hold in Japan.

Measured globally, the contrast between the United States and Japan appears just as striking. Over a quarter of American adults, 28 percent, hold net worths that place them down in the bottom 90 percent of the world's wealth-holders. Only 6.8 percent of adults in Japan live among the world's poorest 90 percent.

Super-Rich Not Counted

How accurately do all these global numbers reflect the actual distribution of the world's household wealth? If anything, notes the UN University study authors, their report understates just how unequal the world's wealth distribution has become. Their base survey data, they explain, "do not reflect the holdings of the super-rich." Their primary official data source for the United States, for instance, "explicitly omits the 'Forbes 400' wealthiest U.S. families." Elsewhere in the world, the authors add, nations only rarely capture the holdings of the super-rich in their official data.

How much of a difference would adding the super-rich into the mix make? In 2000, *Forbes* magazine reports, the world's 492 billionaires held a combined $2.16 trillion in wealth, a sum that amounts to 1.7 percent of the $125.3 trillion in world household wealth identified in the UN University study, or more than the wealth of the world's poorest 1.5 billion people.

[The United Nations] predicted a 'human development disaster' if the world's nations continue to ignore how they distribute . . . the wealth their economies create.

So does all this matter? Should the world's peoples worry about how concentrated the ownership of the world's wealth has become? Until recently, mainstream global economic analysts downplayed, even dismissed, inequality as a problem. These analysts put their faith in economic growth. If economies were growing, they believed, wealth—and social well-being—could eventually percolate all throughout society and eventually improve everyone's standard of living. But two blockbuster reports [in the fall of 2006], one from the United Nations and the other from the World Bank, directly challenged this mainstream indifference to inequality.

Disaster Predicted

[In] September [2005], the UN Human Development 2005 Report predicted a "human development disaster" if the world's nations continue to ignore how they distribute, within their own borders, the wealth their economies create. "Redistributing 1.6 percent of the income of the richest 10 percent of the global population," the report noted, "would provide the $300 billion needed to lift the 1 billion people living on less than a dollar a day out of extreme poverty, at least temporarily." And that shift would soon evolve into a permanent state of affairs, the report added, because "improved distributional equity" would both increase "the size of the economic pie" and enable the poor "to capture a bigger slice of that pie."

Just weeks later, a team of economists and social scientists from the World Bank pounded home the same message. The World Bank's top analysts acknowledged for the first-time ever, as a *BBC News* analysis noted at the time, "that redistribution—as well as economic growth—is needed to end world poverty." Nations can't offer equity of opportunity, stressed Francisco Ferreira, a co-author of the *World Bank Equity and Development* report, without first achieving a healthy measure of equity in distribution. That's because, Ferreira explained, "societies with extreme inequality in wealth generate also extreme inequality in power."

Governing for the Elite

Governments that reflect these extreme inequalities in power, the World Bank economist added, tend to govern not in the public interest, but in the interest of wealthy elites. Other economic and social analysts, meanwhile, have been pointing out that deep economic inequality can have as socially destructive an impact on rich nations as on poor. Affluent and poor people alike in relatively equal "rich" nations, for instance, live longer than affluent and poor people in "rich" nations that tolerate greater inequality.

Japan, the nation with the world's most equal distribution of income and wealth, currently sports the world's longest life expectancy, at 82.2 years, reports the . . . 2006 UN Human Development Report. The developed world's most unequal nation, the United States, now ranks No. 30 on the global life expectancy list, at 77.5 years, despite spending considerably more on health care than any other nation in the world. In 1970, a much more equal United States was in twelfth place on that list.

The authors of the UN University wealth study end their report with a plea for better data. More countries, the authors note, need to be regularly collecting statistics on just who owns what. Without that data, they contend, tracking progress toward a more equal world will be essentially "impossible." But more data may not be what the global struggle against inequality needs most. Data, thanks to this sweeping new study, now abound. The global political will to act on these data, that's another story.

Organizations to Contact

The editors have compiled the following list of organizations concerned with the issues debated in this book. The descriptions are derived from materials provided by the organizations. All have publications or information available for interested readers. The list was compiled on the date of publication of the present volume; the information provided here may change. Be aware that many organizations take several weeks or longer to respond to inquiries, so allow as much time as possible.

Brookings Institution
1775 Massachusetts Ave. NW, Washington, DC   20036
(202) 797-6000 • fax: (202) 797-6004
e-mail: brookinfo@brook.edu
Web site: www.brook.edu

The Brookings Institution is a think tank that conducts research and education in the areas of foreign policy, economics, government, and the social sciences. Its Web site features numerous briefings and publications on the topic of the global economy. Examples include *The WTO and Sustainable Development, Insuring America's Workers in an Age of Offshoring,* and *Do EU Trade Policies Impoverish Developing Countries?*

Earth Island Institute
300 Broadway, Suite 28, San Francisco, CA   94133
(415) 788-3666 • fax: (415) 788-7324
e-mail: earthisland@earthisland.org
Web site: www.earthisland.org

Earth Island Institute's work addresses environmental issues and their relation to such concerns as human rights and economic development in the Third World. The institute's publications include the quarterly *Earth Island Journal.* The articles "Bucking the Corporate Future" and "In Favor of a New Protectionism," are available on its Web site.

50 Years Is Enough Network
3628 Twelfth St. NE, Washington, DC   20017
(202) 463-2265
e-mail: info@50years.org
Web site: www.50years.org

Founded on the fiftieth anniversary of the World Bank and International Monetary Fund, the 50 Years Is Enough Network—the coalitions of more than two hundred antiglobalization groups—is dedicated to reforming the policies and practices of the two international financial institutions. On its Web site the network provides fact sheets and international debt-relief articles, including the fact sheets *Africa Needs Debt Cancellation, Not More IMF Programs* and *IMF/WB Debt Plan: Still Failing After All These Years.*

Friends of the Earth International
PO Box 19199, Amsterdam   1000 gd
  The Netherlands
+31 20 622 1369 • fax: +31 20 639
Web site: www.foei.org

Friends of the Earth is an international advocacy organization dedicated to protecting the planet from environmental degradation; preserving biological, cultural, and ethnic diversity; and empowering citizens to have an influential voice in decisions affecting the quality of their environment. It has a U. S. chapter and produces numerous publications dealing with the environment. Recent publications include *How the World Bank's Energy Framework Sells the Climate and Poor People Short* and *The Tyranny of Free Trade.*

Global Policy Forum (GPF)
777 UN Plaza, Suite 73DG, New York, NY   10017
(212) 557-3161 • fax: (212) 557-3165
e-mail: gpf@globalpolicy.org
Web site: www.globalpolicy.org

Global Policy Forum monitors policy making at the United Nations, promotes accountability of global decisions, educates and mobilizes citizen participation, and advocates on vital issues of international peace and justice. The forum publishes policy papers and the *GPF Newsletter*. On its Web site GPF provides an internal globalization link with subcategories on several topics, including politics, culture, and economics. The Web site provides charts, graphs, and articles, including *Measuring Globalization: Who's Up, Who's Down?*

Global Trade Watch (GTW)
215 Pennsylvania Ave. SE, Washington, DC   20003
(202) 546-4996
e-mail: gtwinfo@citizen.org
Web site: www.tradewatch.org

GTW is a division of the nonprofit public interest group Public Citizen. It promotes democracy by challenging corporate globalization, arguing that today's globalization model is neither an example of random inevitability nor free trade. GTW works on an array of globalization issues, including health and safety, environmental protection, economic justice, and democratic, accountable governance. GTW publishes books, including *Whose Trade Organization? A Comprehensive Guide to the WTO*, and fact sheets and articles, such as *Our World Is Not for Sale*, that are available on its Web site.

Global Water
3600 S. Harbor Blvd., Suite 514, Oxnard, CA   93035
(805) 985-3057 • fax: (805) 985-3688
e-mail: info@globalwater.org
Web site: www.globalwater.org

Global Water is an international nonprofit, nongovernmental organization dedicated to helping to provide clean drinking water for developing countries. The organization provides technical assistance, water supply equipment, and volunteers to help poor countries develop safe and effective water supply programs around the world.

Greenpeace USA
702 H St. NW, Suite 300, Washington, DC   20001

(800) 326-0959
e-mail: info@wdc.greenpeace.org
Web site: www.greenpeace.org

Greenpeace is a global nonprofit organization and advocacy group that focuses on the most crucial worldwide threats to the planet's biodiversity and environment. Its Web site lists numerous environmental position papers and other publications relating to globalization and the environment. Recent publications include *Deadly Subsidies, The US Assault on Biodiversity—The WTO Dispute on GMOs,* and *Trading Away Our Last Ancient Forests.*

International Forum on Globalization (IFG)
1009 General Kennedy Ave. #2, San Francisco, CA   94129
(415) 561-7650 • fax: (415) 561-7651
e-mail: ifg@ifg.org
Web site: www.ifg.org

The International Forum on Globalization is an alliance of sixty leading activists, scholars, economists, researchers, and writers formed to stimulate new thinking, joint activity, and public education in response to economic globalization. IFG publishes various reports, audiotapes, books, and other materials relating to the effects of globalization. Recent publications include *China Copes with Globalization: A Mixed Review* and *Paradigm Wars: Indigenous Peoples' Resistance to Economic Globalization.*

International Monetary Fund (IMF)
700 Nineteenth St. NW, Washington, DC   20431
(202) 623-7000 • fax: (202) 623-4661
e-mail: publicaffairs@imf.org
Web site: www.imf.org

The IMF is an international organization of 184 member countries. It was established to promote international monetary cooperation, exchange stability, and orderly exchange arrangements. IMF fosters economic growth and high levels of employment and provides temporary financial assistance to countries. It publishes the quarterly *Finance & Development* and reports on its activities, including the quarterly *Global Financial Stability Report,* recent issues of which are available on its Web site along with data on IMF finances and individual country reports.

International Water Management Institute (IWMI)
PO Box 2075, Colombo
  Sri Lanka
+94 11 2787404, 2784080 • fax: +94 11 2786854
e-mail: iwmi@cgiar.org
Web site: www.iwmi.cgiar.org

The International Water Management Institute is a nonprofit scientific organization funded by the Consultative Group on International Agricultural Research. IWMI concentrates on water and related land management challenges faced by poor rural communities.

Rand Corporation
1776 Main St., Santa Monica, CA   90407-2138
(310) 393-0411 • fax: (310) 393-4818
Web site: www.rand.org

Rand is a nonprofit think tank that conducts research and analysis on national security, business, education, health, law, and science. Its Web site features a "Hot Topics" section on globalization that provides selected research, commentary, and congressional testimony by Rand experts on the topic.

Sierra Club
85 Second St., 2nd Floor, San Francisco, CA   94105
(415) 977-5500 • fax: (415) 977-5799
e-mail: information@sierraclub.org
Web site: www.sierraclub.org

The Sierra Club is a grassroots environmental organization with more than 750,000 members that works to protect the natural and human environments around the world. It publishes a bimonthly magazine, *Sierra*, a newsletter, and numerous other publications. Its Web site contains reports and analyses of the effects of globalization, including *Taming Globalization for People and the Planet, Globalization Is Heading the Wrong Way,* and *No Globalization Without Representation.*

United Nations Conference on Trade and Development (UNCTAD)

Palais des Nations, 8-14, Av. de la Paix   1211 Geneva 10
    Switzerland
+41 22 917 5809 • fax: +41 22 917 0051
e-mail: info@unctad.org
Web site: www.unctad.org

UNCTAD was established by the United Nations to help integrate developing countries into the world economy. UNCTAD has organized three UN conferences on least developed countries, and its Special Programme for Least Developed, Landlocked and Island Developing Countries promotes the socioeconomic development of these countries through research, policy analysis, and technical assistance. Its Web site contains information about the least developed countries and links to UN reports and other materials relating to trade issues and development.

United Nations Development Programme (UNDP)

1 United Nations Plaza, New York, NY   10017
(212) 906-5000 • fax: (212) 906-5364
Web site: www.undp.org

UNDP funds six thousand projects in more than 150 developing countries and territories. It works with governments, UN agencies, and nongovernmental organizations to enhance self-reliance and promote sustainable human development. Its priorities include improving living standards, protecting the environment, and applying technology to meet human needs. UNDP's publications include the weekly newsletter *UNDP-Flash*, the human development magazine *Choices*, and the annual *UNDP Human Development Report*. On its Web site, UNDP publishes the *Millennium Development Goals*, its annual report, regional data and analysis, speeches and statements, and recent issues of its publications.

**United Nations Educational, Scientific, and
Cultural Organization (UNESCO)**
7, Place de Fontenoy   75352 Paris 07 SP
   France
+33(0)1 45 68 10 00 • fax: +33(0)1 45 67 16 90
e-mail: bpi@unesco.org
Web site: www.unesco.org

UNESCO is a specialized agency of the United Nations that seeks to promote cooperation among member countries in the areas of education, science, culture, and communication. UNESCO is actively pursuing the UN's Millennium Development Goals, which seek to halve the proportion of people living in extreme poverty in developing countries, achieve universal primary education in all countries, eliminate gender disparity in primary and secondary education, help countries implement a national strategy for sustainable development, and reverse current trends in the loss of environmental resources by 2015.

**United Nations Educational, Scientific, and
Cultural Organization (UNESCO) World Water
Assessment Programme**
1, Rue Miollis, Paris   75015
   France
+33 (0)1 45 68 10 00 • fax: +33 (0)1 45 68 58 11
e-mail: wwap@unesco.org
Web site: www.unesco.org/water/wwap

The World Water Assessment Programme is part of UNESCO and is designed to provide information related to global freshwater issues. Every three years, it publishes the *United Nations World Water Development Report*, a comprehensive review that gives an overall picture of the state of the world's freshwater resources and aims to provide decision makers with the tools to implement sustainable use of our water.

World Bank (IBRD)
1818 H St. NW, Washington, DC   20433
(202) 473-1000 • fax: (202) 477-6391
Web site: www.worldbank.org

Formally known as the International Bank for Reconstruction and Development (IBRD), the World Bank seeks to reduce poverty and improve the standards of living of poor people around the world. It promotes sustainable growth and investments in developing countries through loans, technical assistance, and policy guidance. The World Bank publishes books on global issues, including *Global Economic Prospects 2005: Trade, Regionalism, and Development, Privatization in Latin America: Myths and Reality,* and *Intellectual Property and Development: Lessons from Recent Economic Research.* On its Web site, the World Bank provides current development data and programs.

World Health Organization (WHO)
Avenue Appia 20   1211 Geneva 27
  Switzerland
+41 22 791 21 11 • fax: +41 22 791 3111
e-mail: info@who.int
Web site: www.who.int

The World Health Organization is the United Nations' specialized agency for health. Established in 1948, WHO seeks to promote the highest possible level of health for all people. Health is defined in WHO's constitution as a state of complete physical, mental and social well-being and not merely the absence of disease or infirmity. WHO is governed by 193 member countries through the World Health Assembly. WHO's Web site contains a library of WHO reports and publications, as well as links to various world health journals and reports.

World Trade Organization (WTO)
Centre William Rappard, Rue de Lausanne 154   CH-1211
  Geneva 21
  Switzerland

+41 22 739 51 11 • fax: +41 22 731 42 06
e-mail: enquiries@wto.org
Web site: www.wto.org

WTO is a global international organization that establishes rules dealing with the trade between nations. Two WTO agreements have been negotiated and signed by the bulk of the world's trading nations and ratified in their parliaments. The goal of these agreements is to help producers of goods and services, exporters, and importers conduct their business. WTO publishes trade statistics, research and analysis, studies, reports, and the journal *World Trade Review*. Recent publications are available on the WTO Web site.

Worldwatch Institute

1776 Massachusetts Ave. NW, Washington, DC   20036-1904
(202) 452-1999 • fax: (202) 296-7365
e-mail: worldwatch@worldwatch.org
Web site: www.worldwatch.org

Worldwatch is a research organization that analyzes and calls attention to global problems, including environmental concerns such as the loss of cropland, forests, habitat, species, and water supplies. It compiles the annual *State of the World* anthology and publishes the bimonthly magazine *World Watch* and the World Watch Paper Series, which includes *Home Grown: The Case for Local Food in a Global Market* and *Underfed and Overfed: The Global Epidemic of Malnutrition*.

World Water Council (WWC)

Espace Gaymard, 2-4 place d'Arvieux, Marseille   13002
   France
+33 4 91 99 41 00 • fax: +33 4 91 99 41 01
Web site: www.worldwatercouncil.org

The World Water Council was established in 1996 in response to increasing concerns from the global community about world water issues. Its mission is to promote awareness, build political commitment, and trigger action on critical water issues at all levels to facilitate the efficient management and use of water on an environmentally sustainable basis.

Bibliography

Books

John Baffoe-Bonnie and Mohammed Khayum	*Contemporary Economic Issues in Developing Countries.* Westport, CT: Praeger, 2003.
Amy Chua	*World on Fire: How Exporting Free Market Democracy Breeds Ethnic Hatred and Global Instability.* New York: Doubleday, 2002.
Christopher Cramer	*Violence in Developing Countries: War, Memory, Progress.* Bloomington: Indiana University Press, 2007.
Pitou van Dijck and Gerrit Faber	*Developing Countries and the Doha Development Agenda of the WTO.* New York: Routledge, 2006.
Douglas A. Irwin	*Free Trade Under Fire.* Princeton, NJ: Princeton University Press, 2005.
Robert A. Isaak	*The Globalization Gap: How the Rich Get Richer and the Poor Get Left Further Behind.* Upper Saddle River, NJ: Prentice-Hall/Financial Times, 2005.
William W. Lewis	*The Power of Productivity: Wealth, Poverty, and the Threat to Global Security.* Chicago: University of Chicago Press, 2004.
Paul Mason	*Poverty.* Oxford, UK: Heinemann Library, 2006.

| Alex F. McCalla and John Nash, eds. | *Reforming Agricultural Trade for Developing Countries.* Washington, DC: World Bank, 2007. |

Gordon McGranahan and Frank Murray | *Air Pollution and Health in Rapidly Developing Countries.* Sterling, VA: Earthscan, 2003.

David Pearce, Corin Pearce, Charles Palmer, and Edward Elgar, eds. | *Valuing the Environment in Developing Countries: Case Studies.* Northhampton, MA: Edward Elgar, 2007.

Sumit Roy | *Globalisation, ICT and Developing Nations: Challenges in the Information Age.* New Delhi, India: Sage 2005.

Jeffrey Sachs | *The End of Poverty: Economic Possibilities for Our Time.* New York: Penguin, 2005.

Bertram I. Spector, ed. | *Fighting Corruption in Developing Countries: Strategies and Analysis.* Bloomfield, CT: Kumarian, 2005.

Joseph Stiglitz | *Globalization and Its Discontents.* New York: Norton, 2002.

Ernest J. Wilson III | *The Information Revolution and Developing Countries.* Cambridge, MA: MIT Press, 2004.

Periodicals

America | "Thanksgiving and World Hunger," November 22, 2004.

Frederik Balfour, Laura Cohn, and Nandini Lakshman — "In Asia, a Hot Market for Carbon," *BusinessWeek*, December 12, 2005.

Mike Brown and Chris Breitenberg — "Declaring War on a Brutal Killer: Corruption and World Poverty Are Inextricably Linked," *For a Change*, June/July 2006.

BusinessWeek Online — "Bill Gates Battles Deadlier Bugs," October 9, 2002. www.businesseweek.com.

Canada and the World Backgrounder — "Weapons of Mass Salvation," September 2003.

David Dollar and Aart Kraay — "Spreading the Wealth," *Foreign Affairs*, January/February 2002.

Economist — "Emerging at Last," September 16, 2006.

Economist — "Making Poverty History," December 18, 2004.

Economist — "Not Yet, Say the Arabs; Arabs and Democracy," July 22, 2006.

Rana Foroohar — ". . . Neither Is the State; a Dissenting View: Efforts to Drive Development and Smooth Out Income Disparities by Fiat Have Proved to Be Far Less Efficient than the Market," *Newsweek*, December 26, 2005–January 2, 2006.

Mary Jane Freeman	"UNDP Report: A Needless Decade of Despair: Developing Nations Are Dying," *Executive Intelligence Review*, August 1, 2003.
Geographical	"The Killer Inside: While the West Tries to Work Out How to Clean Up the Air in Its Cities, More and More People in the Developing World Are Being Killed by Indoor Air Pollution," April 2004. www.geographical.co.uk.
Global Agenda	"A Smaller World; World Population Growth: Slowing Down?" March 13, 2002.
Global Agenda	"Whatever It Takes; Report on Global Poverty; Sachs's Solutions," January 18, 2005.
August Gribbin	"Overpopulated Megacities Face Frightening Future," *Insight on the News*, August 21, 2000.
Janet Larsen	"A Burgeoning World Population," *USA Today* magazine, March 2005.
Matthew C. Mahutga	"The Persistence of Structural Inequality? A Network Analysis of International Trade, 1965–2000," *Social Forces*, June 2006.
Floyd Norris	"Maybe Developing Nations Are Not Emerging but Have Emerged," *New York Times*, December 30, 2006.

Oil and Gas Journal	"Developing Countries Make Strides to Cut GHG Emissions," January 13, 2003.
Robert B. Reich	"A Case for Tailoring—and Slowing—Free Trade in Poor Nations," *New York Times*, March 31, 2006.
Samanta Sen	"Environment: Developing World Fast Running Out of Water," *Environment Bulletin*, March 26, 2001.
Priya Shetty	"Developing Nations 'Must Fight Chronic Diseases,'" *SciDev.Net*, October 5, 2005.
Jim Shultz	"People Power: Globalization Resistance Brings Down a President," *New Internationalist*, December 2003.
Michele G. Sullivan	"Preventable Conditions Kill 10.6 Million Children: Most of These Causes Can Be Addressed Right Now with Inexpensive and Easy Interventions That Work," *Family Practice News*, June 1, 2005.

Index

Y

Youth
   chronic hunger among, 36
   in developing nations, globalization increases opportunities for, 78–83
   early marriage/childbearing among, 81–82

Z

Zakaria, Fareed, 121

Zarqawi, Abu Musab, 106, 108–109

Zedillo, Ernesto, 68

Zinc deficiency, 32